In times past, you either occupied pulpit or pew ... served the Church or attended church...viewed your vocation as sacred or secular. In recent decades, however, lay people have rediscovered their calling to *be* the Church. As such, they desire to assume the ministries of witnessing, fellowship, and service. How can this come about in your local church? John Stott believes that a practical recovery of the true biblical functions for leaders and lay people will produce the every-member ministry so central to New Testament teaching. Whatever your present role, this lively and provocative study will help you clarify your God-given responsibilities in the Body of Christ.

By John Stott

John Stott

**Helping your church
become a caring
community**

ONE
PEOPLE

Expanded & Updated

Fleming H. Revell Company
Old Tappan, New Jersey

Library of Congress Cataloging in Publication Data
Stott, John R. W.
One people.
Bibliography: p.
1. Laity.   2. Lay ministry.   I. Title.
BV4525.S67   1982   253   82-9092
ISBN 0-8007-5099-3   AACR2

Contents

Foreword

The decade of the 1960s was a momentous period in modern church history. During the ferment of those days, there came an awakening of the concept of the laity in the church. Dr. Stott's book, *One People,* was on the cutting edge of that awakening, calling for a return to the biblical pattern of the church as a ministering community, teaching that every member of Christ's Body is called and empowered by God's Spirit to be a fruitful minister.

The revival of that concept has brought new life and vigor to the churches of the western world. Virtually every pastor has been made to rethink the roles of the so-called laity and clergy. This breath of fresh air has brought new excitement and not a few tensions.

Now with the reissue of *One People,* I am both pleased and honored to have been asked by the publishers to contribute a chapter, sharing some of the growth experiences of Long Hill Chapel. It is my fervent hope that this book will present a new challenge to God's people in North America.

Paul F. Bubna
Senior Pastor
Long Hill Chapel
Chatham, New Jersey

Preface

The substance of this book was first used in the annual Pastoral Theology lectures commissioned by the Divinity Faculty of the University of Durham, England. They were delivered in February 1968 and published in 1969. Having been invited to take "the theology of the laity" as my topic, what concerned me throughout was the development of those harmonious relationships between clergy and laity, or pastors and people, which are essential both to biblical obedience and to the health of the Church. Inevitably I drew on my parochial experience at All Souls Church, Langham Place, London. If the personal references jar on my readers, I ask them to believe that their purpose is not self-advertisement, but rather a desire to "ground" theories in an actual real-life situation. To be sure, church life in central London differs from suburban and rural contexts. Nevertheless, if the principles unfolded here are as biblical as I believe them to be, they can be adapted to church life in any situation.

In the fourteen years which have elapsed since 1968, great changes have taken place in the world, in the Church at large, and at All Souls Church. Let me elaborate on these.

The 1960s were a decade of turbulent change, even of revolution. The "wind of change," which Harold McMillan declared in 1960 to be blowing through Africa, proved to be a gale of global proportions. That year the Belgian Congo gained its independence (becoming Zaire in 1971). Uganda, Kenya and Tanzania

9

obtained their national independence in 1962, '63, and '64 respectively. The Free Speech Movement erupted on the Berkeley campus in 1964. Racial tension in the United States flared up into race riots between 1965 and 1968. In 1968 the "Prague Spring," which sought to put a human face on Communism, blossomed briefly, only to wither and die, crushed by the brutality of Soviet tanks. In 1968 French students and workers took to the barricades in the streets of Paris. It was an era of protest against authoritarianism and of demand for responsible participation in the government of country, industry, and university. It was essentially a "lay" movement, a refusal to kowtow to an autocracy of "professionals."

The Church did not escape this mood. Nor should it have. Christianity has been a lay movement from the beginning, and every renewal or revival in Church history has been at least partly a reassertion of the rights and duties of the lay people over against the powers usurped by the hierarchy. The Second Vatican Council (1962–65) at least began to concede to Roman Catholic laity privileges which they had long been denied. Lay Bible reading, for example, which had for centuries been discouraged and in some countries actually forbidden, was now enjoined on all.

Then the Charismatic Movement, which had begun in the fifties, became an almost universal phenomenon in both the Roman Catholic and the Protestant Churches. True, serious theological questions remain, especially about the distinctively Pentecostal doctrines of Spirit-baptism and of the charismata (see my *Baptism and Fullness* for an introductory critique). Nevertheless, all of us must welcome the impetus which the movement has given to a recovery of the New Testament doctrine of the Church as the Body of Christ, whose members are called to exercise their gifts in ministry and to serve one another in mutual respect and love.

Another important trend in the Church of the seventies has been the growing women's movement, and in particular the debate about women's ministry. Unfortunately, the issues became clouded by Catholic notions of "priesthood" and "ordination," and the wrong question was (and is) often asked, "Can a woman be a priest?" Unfortunately also, a sterile polarization has developed. On the one hand, there is an extreme feminism which refuses to recognize either that there is any significant differentiation of sexual characteristics and roles or that the New Testament writers have any contemporary authority, or both. On the other hand, there is a conservative backlash which is cruelly oppressive because it denies women any outlets for service. It is to be hoped that we shall find in the eighties a better and more biblically balanced position, which encourages women to exercise their God-given gifts in ministry, and at the same time recognizes male "headship" or caring responsibility as the God-ordained context in which women find their true liberation and fulfillment.

From these movements for change in the world and the Church I come back to All Souls Church in London. In 1975, after twenty-five years as rector (i.e. senior pastor), I resigned and was replaced by Michael Baughen, who had already taken over the leadership of the church—in fact though not yet in + Bethel? title—five years earlier. Under his gifted and dynamic pastoral guidance, the church has gone from strength to strength, and since I have remained for six months every year an active member of the pastoral team, although called "Rector Emeritus," I have been able to watch the developments. Our biblical theology of lay ministry has not changed, but it has been more thoroughly implemented. Since the population of London is extremely unstable, the All Souls congregation keeps changing too. Students stay for three years and move away. Young professional people are promoted to more responsible jobs in the provinces. Couples, who begin their married life in a small apartment, soon go off in search of a house with a backyard where their children can play in safety. Older people retire and leave the city. As a result, the church almost resembles the transit lounge of an international airport, so continuous is the coming and going. This fact has increasingly influenced our thinking. Since our church members stay only for an average of two or three years, we see the need to exploit this opportunity to train them while we have them. So Michael Baughen appointed Andrew Cornes as Director of Training, and he has developed a comprehensive program. Fellowship Groups have expanded too. There were nearly fifty when I resigned; now there are nearly eighty, and more care is given to the training and pastoral oversight of their leaders.

In preparing a second edition of this book, I had therefore to ask myself how it should reflect these changes. After careful thought I decided to leave the book's four chapters more or less untouched. Integrity seemed to demand this, partly because the lectures were given in a particular historical context, and partly because it did not seem appropriate to incorporate into my text the changes for which my colleagues have been responsible. So what I have done is to add updating postscripts to Chapters 3 and 4. In the former I have described the program which Andrew Cornes as Director of Training has initiated, and in the latter the developments of the Fellowship Groups which have taken place under the leadership of Richard Inwood, Director of Pastoring. All the members of our pastoral staff enormously enjoy working together, for teamwork enables us to capitalize one another's strengths and compensate for one another's weaknesses. We also enjoy welcoming other pastors, at Michael Baughen's invitation, to an annual "Alongside Week," which gives them the opportunity to see and share what we are seeking under God to do together.

I am very glad that the publishers decided to invite Paul F. Bubna to contribute an additional chapter from a North American perspective, and I am grateful for what he has written.

Finally, I have two apologies to make. The first is for the use of transliterated Greek words. I have retained them because it seems to me that Christian people should be familiar with some of the common New Testament words which have a particular flavor of their own. All of us nowadays include in our vocabulary words of Greek origin like antibiotic, psychosomatic and stereophonic. We do not jib at them. Children learn in their school botany lessons about photosynthesis; journalists love to write about euphoria and syndromes; and church leaders lose no opportunity to remind us of the eschatological significance of ecumenicity! So I hope that words like *ecclesia, diakonia, marturia,* and *koinonia* will not deter the reader, even if they are not yet in everyday parlance.

To American readers I have a further apology to make, namely that a number of my allusions are inevitably to the English, and indeed the Anglican, scene. Perhaps I need to explain that the Church of England is the English equivalent of the American Episcopal Church, that the "Thirty-Nine Articles" date from 1562 and are still one of the doctrinal standards of Anglican or Episcopal churches, and that the "Lambeth Conference" brings together, approximately every ten years, all the diocesan bishops of the Anglican Communion. The first Lambeth Conference was held in 1888, and the post-war conferences have taken place in 1948, 1958, 1968, and 1978.

John Stott
December 1981

Introduction
The Resurgence of the Laity

The Church constantly changes. Nowhere does this seem more evident than in contemporary attitudes toward the laity. In every part of the Christian Church lay people are coming into their own.

There have been notable lay movements before, for example, in the Middle Ages and during the Reformation; and the lay initiative which led to the founding of great international youth and missionary movements in the nineteenth century has not yet spent its force. But these were spontaneous, the upsurge of lay energy from below, sometimes tolerated by church leaders only because they had no alternative. Today, however, toleration is being superseded by encouragement, reluctance by enthusiasm. Lay people are being taken seriously because there is a growing recognition of their true place in the Church.

Contrast this attitude with that expressed in the Encyclical of Pope Pius X in 1906 entitled *Vehementer Nos:* "As for the masses, they have no other right than that of letting themselves be led, and of following their pastors as a docile flock."

Only a few years ago Sir Kenneth Grubb assessed the Anglican position by saying, "The Church of England does not give a strong impression of being interested in its laity: it seems either to ride them or to fear them."[1]

Such patronizing sentiments are seldom expressed now, however. On the contrary, a statement from the 1958 Lambeth Conference said, "There is a growing recognition today that too sharp a distinction has been made between clergy and laity,"[2] and "there is need for a better theology of the laity."[3]

Why this increasing prominence of the lay person in the contemporary Church? Several reasons suggest themselves.

First, the sociological factor. In England, between 1851 and 1966 there was a fall in the ratio of clergy to people from 1 in 1,000 to 1 in 2,500. This combination of more people and fewer pastors is a contributory factor in the current drift from the churches. Many overworked clergy, who previously held the ecclesiastical reins tightly in their own hands, are now obliged to seek the help of the laity. Tom Allan refers to them as "the unemployed of the Church,"[4] but now many are being found employment. As Hendrik Kraemer puts it, the laity had before "existed mainly as frozen credits"; now they are being unfrozen and put into circulation. We cannot stop there, however, for to borrow another of Kraemer's metaphors, the laity are "not primarily an insufficiently tapped reservoir of man-power."[5]

Secondly, the pragmatic reason. Although this is not a worthy argument, the plain fact is that if we do not give lay people—perhaps especially the men—man-sized jobs to do, we shall lose them, at least in their spare time, to the Masons or Rotary or one of the other secular voluntary services, or even one of the cults, all of whom are better at giving responsible positions to gifted people than most churches have ever been.[6] This is not to say that Christians should not be involved in community service. They should. When such involvement is recognized as part of the Christian calling and has the supporting encouragement of the local church, it is good and right. But when it is undertaken only *faute de mieux,* from a sense of frustrated uselessness in the church, something has gone sadly wrong.

Canon Max Warren made this point well.[7] He compared the revival movement in East Africa, which has stayed inside the Church, with the separatist groups in South Africa, of which at that time there were more than 1,300. They have been described by Dr. (later Bishop) B.G.M. Sundkler in his *Bantu Prophets in South Africa,* and from this study Canon Warren made a number of significant points. The first is that "it is impossible to condemn the African for being separatist when he is treated as a separated person." He continued: "The fact that in addition to being separated within the Church he was subordinated as well, and so was unable to exercise either initiative or authority, powerfully conduced to the act of formal separation." Therefore, "the problem of how to provide adequate scope for initiative and leadership, the problem of 'the layman,' remains one of the more outstanding of the tasks confronting the Church in Africa." The same is true throughout the world.

Thirdly, the spirit of the age. The Church has not escaped the effects of the social and political revolution which has engulfed the world in this century, and has brought maturity and a sense of responsibility to large numbers of ordinary citizens. Compulsory secondary education and the increasing availability of higher education, the spread of democracy and with it of universal adult suffrage, the emancipation of "the workers" in both communist and capitalist forms, the trades' union movement, the global revolt against privilege, authoritarianism and every kind of establishment, and the insistence upon egalitarian rights are all straws in the same wind. To this modern outlook the Church often appeared to be a redoubtable bastion of the old order, reactionary and resistant to change, while its hierarchical structure seemed to some like an antique relic of the feudalism which was otherwise discarded in the Middle Ages. But now "participatory democracy" is being sought in industry as well as in local and national government, and the Church which should have set an example in this development finds itself obliged to follow where others are leading.

These are three practical reasons for the greater participation of lay people in the life and work of the Church—need, fear, and the spirit of the age. They are sound reasons too, so far as they go, but inadequate. The real reason for expecting the laity to be responsible, active and constructive church members is biblical not pragmatic, grounded on theological principle, not on expediency. It is neither because the clergy need the laity to help them, nor because the laity want to be of use, nor because the world now thinks this way, but because God himself has revealed it as his will. Moreover, the only way in which the laity will come to see and accept their inalienable rights and duties in the Church is that they come to recognize them in the Word of God as the will of God for the people of God.

So *fourthly,* and most important of all, there is *the biblical argument.* We have already seen that it is impossible to talk about laity without also talking about clergy. We must now see that it is impossible to talk about either without talking about the Church to which they both belong. "Fundamentally," wrote Yves Congar, "there can be only one valid theology of the laity: a total ecclesiology."[8] It is safe to say that unbalanced notions about either clergy or laity are due to unbalanced notions of the Church. Indeed, to be more precise, too low a view of laity is due to too high a view of clergy, and too high a view of clergy is due to too low a view of the Church.

It may be helpful if at this stage I sketch out the ground which I hope to cover in this book.

In the first chapter we shall consider some of the main emphases in the biblical doctrine of the Church, the *ecclesia,* particularly in connection with the relations between clergy and laity.

In the second chapter I shall try to outline the four kinds of relationship which at various times have existed between clergy and laity. I shall urge that clergy are called to ministry (*dia-*

konia), and that therefore the true and proper relationship of clergy to laity is a *serving* relationship.

In Chapter 3 this general principle will be worked out in detail and in practice. We shall see that the chief way in which the clergy are to serve the laity is in helping to teach and train them for their life, work and especially witness (*maturia*) in the world. In other words the *diakonia,* service, of the clergy is subservient to the *marturia* of the laity. In unfolding this theme, I will share with you some of our experience in London both of an annual training program for the equipment of "Commissioned Workers" and of their varied service in the parish. As I do so, I shall describe the scheme so far as possible through their eyes as well as mine, since I shall draw on their answers to a questionnaire submitted to them.

In Chapter 4, we shall move on from the relations between clergy and laity to the wider field of the relations of church members to one another in the fellowship of the Church. I shall attempt to unfold what the Bible means by *koinonia,* fellowship, and to explore how it should be expressed in the local congregation. This will involve an examination of "Fellowship Groups," both the biblical ideal and the actual reality.

1

The Christian Assembly
(*ecclesia*)

The question we must ask in this first chapter is: what is the Church?

The Church is a people, a community of people, who owe their existence, their solidarity, and their corporate distinctness from other communities to one thing only—the call of God.

It all began with Abraham, called by God to leave his own country and kindred in order to be given another country and another kindred, in order to be made a great people through whom all peoples on earth would be blessed. Several times this covenant of grace was confirmed to Abraham, that through his descendants all earth's nations would be blessed.[1] It was then further confirmed to Abraham's son Isaac and to Isaac's son Jacob. But Jacob died in captivity. So did his distinguished son Joseph. Indeed Genesis ends with the prosaic information that after Joseph died, he was embalmed and "put in a coffin in Egypt."[2]

But there was a great leap forward in the fulfillment of God's promise when through Moses, descended from Jacob's son Levi, he rescued the people from their slavery. "When Israel was a

child, I loved him, and out of Egypt I called my son."[3] Three
months after the Exodus they entered the wilderness of Sinai,
and the Lord told Moses to say to the people:

> You have seen . . . how I bore you on eagles' wings and brought
> you to myself. Now therefore, if you will obey my voice and keep
> my covenant, you shall be my own possession among all peoples;
> for all the earth is mine, and you shall be to me a kingdom of
> priests and a holy nation.[4]

So the covenant was ratified, the law given, the tabernacle worship begun. Later the promised land was conquered, and later
still the monarchy established. But it all ended in disaster. God's
people broke his covenant, rejected his law and despised his
prophets, until there was no remedy. The judgment of God fell
upon them, and the second (or Babylonian) captivity began.

Yet God did not abandon his people. In due course, true to his
promise to bless them, he called them out of Babylon, as he had
called them out of Egypt, and he restored them to their own land.
As God said through Jeremiah:

> Therefore, behold, the days are coming, says the Lord, when it
> shall no longer be said, "As the Lord lives who brought up the
> people of Israel out of the land of Egypt," but "As the Lord lives
> who brought up the people of Israel out of the north country and
> out of all the countries where he had driven them." For I will bring
> them back to their own land which I gave to their fathers.[5]

But God had also promised through his people to bless all the
nations of the earth. And this came to pass through Christ. For
God's call into the land of Canaan first of Abraham's family
from Ur and from Haran, then of Jacob's descendants from
Egypt, and then of the remnant of Judah from Babylon all fore-
shadowed a better call, a greater redemption, and a richer inheritance. Through the death and resurrection of Christ, God's purpose is to call out of the world a people for himself, to redeem

them from sin, and to cause them to inherit his promises of salvation.

So the Church is God's people, his *ecclesia,* called out of the world to be his, and existing as a separate entity solely because of his call. The New Testament insists strongly upon this fact. God has called us "into the fellowship of his Son Jesus Christ our Lord," called us "to belong to Jesus Christ."[6] This divine call is "a holy calling," a calling "in holiness."[7] God calls us to be holy as he is holy, and "to lead a life worthy of the calling" to which we have been called,[8] so that by the sanctifying power of the Holy Spirit we may become in character and conduct what we already are in status, namely "saints," the holy, the distinct, the separate, the special people of God.[9]

But God's call is not intended to withdraw the Church out of the world into pietism. As Bishop Lesslie Newbigin puts it, "The Church . . . is a community *in via,* on its way to the ends of the earth and to the end of time." Again,

> the Church is the pilgrim people of God. It is on the move—hastening to the ends of the earth to beseech all men to be reconciled to God, and hastening to the end of time to meet its Lord who will gather all into one.

It is for this reason, he argues, that the Church "cannot be understood rightly except in a perspective which is at once missionary and eschatological."[10] So, the New Testament authors declare, the God who has called us out of the world sends us back into the world:

> You are a chosen race, a royal priesthood, a holy nation, God's own people, that you may declare the wonderful deeds of him who called you out of darkness into his marvelous light.[11]

He has also called us like Christ to suffer in the world unjustly, and through suffering he has called us "to his eternal glory in Christ."[12]

Such is the Church, God's people, called out of the world to himself, called to holiness, called to mission, called to suffering, and called through suffering to glory.

GOD'S CHURCH IS ONE CHURCH

And this calling of the Church is the calling of the whole Church, and of every member of the Church, without any distinction or partiality. Previously, God's call had been to Abraham and his descendants, to physical, national Israel, and the Gentiles had been "alienated from the commonwealth of Israel, and strangers to the covenants of promise."[13] Yet the promise to Abraham included an ultimate blessing for all the nations. So Paul could write to the Ephesians:

> But now in Christ Jesus you who once were far off have been brought near in the blood of Christ. For he is our peace, who has made us both one, and has broken down the dividing wall of hostility, by abolishing in his flesh the law of commandments and ordinances, that he might create in himself one new man in place of the two, so making peace, and might reconcile us both to God in one body through the cross, thereby bringing the hostility to an end.[14]

We must not miss the apostle's reference to an abolition and a creation. God abolished that aspect of the law which made Israel a separate people, and he created "one new man."

And this one new humanity, which is the Church, is a marvelously comprehensive community. Christ has abolished more barriers than that of race or nationality; he has abolished those of class and sex as well: "there is neither Jew nor Greek, there is neither slave nor free, there is neither male nor female; for you are all one in Christ Jesus."[15] Thus the days of discrimination are over. The new humanity Christ has created in the Church tolerates no distinction of race, rank, or sex. This does not mean that Christian equality is a synonym for anarchy, since the same apostle who asserts it also tells wives to be subject to their husbands and servants to their masters, but rather that all spiritual privilege before God has been eliminated:

> For there is no distinction . . . the same Lord is Lord of all and bestows his riches upon all who call upon him. For "everyone who calls upon the name of the Lord will be saved."[16]

As a result all Christian believers, whether Jew or Gentile, male or female, slave or freeman, educated Greek or uncouth barbarian or Scythian, are "fellow citizens with the saints and members of the household of God," and again "fellow heirs, members of the same body, and partakers of the promise in Christ Jesus through the gospel."[17] Paul's use in these verses of four Greek compounds which might be rendered "fellow citizens," "fellow heirs," "fellow members," and "fellow partakers"[18] enforces as clearly and strongly as any words could the undifferentiated, common participation of all God's people in all the blessings of the gospel. He is teaching the same truth in his catalog of unities in Ephesians 4:4–6, that

> there is one body and one Spirit, just as you were called to the one hope that belongs to your call, one Lord, one faith, one baptism, one God and Father of us all, who is above all and through all and in all.

But what is the relevance of this to a book about the laity? Why have I thought it necessary to reassert this abolition of privilege and this creation of one new humanity with equal rights and equal privileges? For this reason: it is only against the background of the equality and unity of the people of God that the real scandal of clericalism may be seen. What clericalism always does, by concentrating power and privilege in the hands of the clergy, is at least to obscure and at worst to annul the essential oneness of the people of God. Extreme forms of clericalism dare to reintroduce the notion of privilege into the only human community in which it has been abolished. Where Christ has made out of two one, the clerical mind makes two again, the one higher and the other lower, the one active and the other passive, the one really important because vital to the life of the Church, the other not vital and therefore less important. I do not hesitate to say that to interpret the Church in terms of a privileged clerical caste or hierarchical structure is to destroy the New Testament doctrine of the Church.

But we have no liberty to interpret "Church" in terms of "clergy," however easy it is for the clerical mind to lapse into this way of thinking. In order to demonstrate this, we shall review some of the chief biblical images of the Church. These are many and varied, and rich in implication. We cannot submit them to an exhaustive examination, but we can consider them with sufficient care to establish this point: every biblical image of the Church illumines the relations of God's people to himself in Christ and/or to each other. Little if any attention is paid to the clergy as a third party distinct from either. In other words, in revealing the nature and work of the Church, the overwhelming preoccupation of the New Testament is not with the status of the clergy, nor with clergy-laity relations, but with the whole people of God in their relations to him and to each other, the unique people who have been called by his grace to be his inheritance and his ambassador in the world.

METAPHORS OF THE CHURCH

Three of the most picturesque images of the Church are taken over by the New Testament from the Old. They represent God's people as his bride, his vineyard, and his flock. They all highlight the direct relationship which God has established with his people and which they enjoy with him.

God looked upon Israel in her maidenhood, betrothed her to himself as his bride and entered into a marriage covenant with her.[19] He then had to keep complaining of her unfaithfulness, her acts of adultery and even her promiscuity.[20]

God brought a vine out of Egypt and planted it in Canaan, "a very fertile hill." There it took root and filled the land. He built a watchtower from which to guard it and a wine-vat to prepare for the vintage. And he looked for it to yield grapes of righteousness, but it yielded only the wild grapes of injustice and oppression. So he made his vineyard a waste.[21]

Again, God was the Shepherd of Israel. He led Joseph like a flock. As he had redeemed them from Egypt, "lifted them up and carried them all the days of old," so after the Babylonian captivity he would gather the lambs in his arms and gently lead those with young.[22]

Each image stresses God's direct and purposeful dealings with his people as a people, his sovereign, saving initiative toward them. He chose Israel as his bride, he planted his vineyard, he shepherded his flock. And when Jesus boldly reapplied the metaphors to himself, he emphasized even more strongly the personal relationship which each implied.

He was the Bridegroom, whose presence with the wedding guests made fasting inappropriate.[23] Paul developed the metaphor in greater detail with reference to Christ's loving self-sacrifice for the Church. His headship over her and his final purpose for her, that she should be presented before him "in splendor, without spot or wrinkle or any such thing."[24] At the end of the Revelation we first hear that "the marriage of the Lamb has come, and his Bride has made herself ready" and then see "the holy city, new Jerusalem, coming down out of heaven from God, prepared as a bride adorned for her husband."[25]

Jesus took up the image of the vineyard in his Parable of the

Wicked Husbandmen,[26] but he also extended it, for he claimed to be the Vine itself, whose branches were dependent for their fruitfulness both on their abiding in him and on their being pruned by the vinedresser.[27]

And Jesus called himself "the Good Shepherd," going out into the wilderness to seek and to save even one lost sheep, laying down his life for his sheep, leading them out into good pasture and protecting them from the wolves.[28]

The four other principal metaphors of the Church in the Bible also illumine the relationship which God has established with his people, although they carry further implications as well.

First, God's people are a *kingdom,* the sphere of his rule, "his dominion."[29] The original Israelite theocracy, which was repudiated when the people asked for a king like the heathen nations, has been recovered and spiritualized through Christ. In saving us God "has delivered us from the dominion of darkness and transferred us to the kingdom of his beloved Son."[30] And Christ exercises his rule in his people through his Spirit, "for the kingdom of God does not mean food and drink but righteousness and peace and joy in the Holy Spirit."[31]

Next, God's people are his *household* or *family.* What was dimly adumbrated in the Old Testament, where Israel was named God's son,[32] is fully worked out in the New. In Christ, God begets us again, makes us his children, adopts us into his family, and sends his Spirit into our hearts that we may call him "Abba Father."[33] Much of the Christian life is determined, as Jesus taught, by this intimate, filial relationship with God. We are to take no anxious thought even for the material necessities of life, because our Heavenly Father knows our needs. We are rather to occupy ourselves with him, with his kingdom, and his righteousness, to commit ourselves and our affairs to him, to trust him to take care of us, and all we need will be given us.[34]

Thirdly, God's people are a *building* "not made with hands," a building which God is himself constructing, the rebuilt spiritual temple, with Jesus Christ as the only foundation as witnessed to by apostles and prophets, and the Holy Spirit as the shechinah presence in the sanctuary.[35]

Fourthly, God's people are the *body of Christ,* the most prominent image in Paul's letters and the only one with no Old Testament equivalent, with Christ as the Head to rule and nourish his body and the Holy Spirit as the breath to animate it.[36]

But each of these four pictures does more than illumine the relation between God and his people. It goes further and illustrates also the mutual relations and duties which God's people have. We are fellow citizens of the Kingdom, brothers and sisters in the Family, living stones being built into the spiritual house, and above all members of Christ's Body, not only receiving life and direction from the Head, but ourselves actively functioning and interdependent, and therefore forbidden either to despise or to envy one another.[37]

MANY METAPHORS—ONE MESSAGE

All this wealth of metaphor points in the same direction. In each image the stress is *either* on God's gracious initiative as Husband, Shepherd, King, Father, Builder, etc., *or* on his people as a redeemed community both in relation to him as his Bride, Flock, Family, Body, etc., and in relation to each other as branches in the same Vine, sheep in the same Flock, children in the same Family, members of the same Body. No metaphor stands or falls by the inclusion of the clergy. This is simply not how the Bible thinks about the Church.

It is perfectly true that Paul likens himself to the best man at the wedding, as did John the Baptist before him.[38] He also speaks of the teaching ministry of himself and Apollos in Corinth in terms of planting and watering the seed in God's field and of laying the foundation and erecting the superstructure of God's building.[39] Similarly, the ministers of the Church are described as under-shepherds to whom the care of the Flock is entrusted,[40] as heralds of the Kingdom, as stewards of the Household, and even sometimes as nursemaids in the Family.[41] It is true also that, although every Christian in the Church is a member of Christ's Body with a function to perform, yet some organs appear to have a more important function than others, for instance the head than the feet and the eye than the hand,[42] although each needs the other and cannot dispense with it.

Nevertheless, every one of these details represents an appendix to the metaphor. The metaphor stands complete without them and, strictly speaking, is independent of them. They have a part to play, but it is a subsidiary part and, one might add, a dispensable part. A best man can be very useful at a wedding, but the bride and bridegroom can marry without one. Stewards and nursemaids are valuable in a home, but a father will not let his children starve for lack of them. No. The truths of central importance which all these church metaphors underline are God's gracious dealings with his people and their responsive duties to him and to each other.

The essential unity of the Church, originating in the call of God and illustrated in the metaphors of Scripture, leads us to this conclusion: the responsibilities which God has entrusted to his Church he has entrusted to his *whole* Church. What are they? "Once you were no people," Peter writes, "but now you are God's people." And God's people, he further explains, are both a *priestly* people, to offer to him the acceptable, spiritual sacrifices of praise and prayer, and a *missionary* people, to declare to others the excellences of their God, the God who has called them into his marvelous light and has had mercy upon them.[43] In brief, God's people are intended to be a worshipping and witnessing community. And both these duties belong to the whole Church as the Church. The clergy cannot monopolize them; nor can the laity escape them. Neither clergy nor laity can delegate them to the other; there is no possibility of worship or witness by proxy.

To insist upon this is a healthy corrective to the exaggerated clericalism which has too often and too long kept the laity in subjection and condemned them to a position of inferiority and in-activity. Clericalism is due to a distorted image of the Church. Certainly, God calls clergy to an important work, but their position is always subordinate to that of the Church as a whole, God's own redeemed community. The laity will only find their rightful place in the Church when the simple truth is recognized that the clergy are there to serve the Church, not the Church the clergy. In order to gain recognition for this truth, we must recover the biblical doctrine of the Church as the people of God, and in particular these truths—that in all matters of status and privilege God's people are by God's call one and undifferentiated, and that the offering of worship to God and the bearing of witness to the world are the inalienable right and duty of this one people, the whole Church, clergy and laity together.

2

The Christian Ministry

(*diakonia*)

We began with the Church, the whole people of God, because this is the preoccupation of Scripture. The story Scripture tells is the story of a people called by God to be distinct from other peoples, the story of this people's varied fortunes according to their varied reactions to the divine call. But everywhere the principal interest is in the people as a unity, and in the God who repeatedly says to them: "I will be your God, and you shall be my people." The distinctive character of every member of the Church of God is not something which may make him different from his fellow Church members, but his very membership of Christ and of Christ's Church, which makes him different from the rest of mankind. And because God's people are different, "holy," they are called to exhibit their difference in their behavior. "I am the Lord your God. You shall not do as they do in the land of Egypt, where you dwelt, and you shall not do as they do in the land of Canaan, to which I am bringing you. You shall not walk in their statutes. You shall do my ordinances and keep my statutes and walk in them. I am the Lord your God."[1] Jesus said much the same thing to His disciples, the nucleus of the new Israel: "You know that the rulers of the Gentiles lord it over them, and their great men exercise authority over them. It shall not be so among you."[2] And the same divine call to be different, to be holy, is heard in the Epistles: "You must no longer live as the Gentiles do."[3]

This then is the basic difference of which God's people are aware. The differentiation is not in the Church, but from the world. They are one with each other but separate from the world because holy unto the Lord.

Nevertheless, within the undifferentiated unity of the people of God differences do exist—differences which relate not to their standing before God but to their function in the community.[4] This contrast between unity and diversity is drawn by the apostle Paul in his letters at least three times, and on each occasion he makes use of the analogy of a single human body consisting of many parts. For example,

> As in one body we have many members, and all the members do not have the same function, so we, though many, are one body in Christ, and individually members one of another. Having gifts that differ according to the grace given to us, let us use them.[5]

The most elaborate exposition of this combination of unity and diversity is in 1 Corinthians 12. The chapter begins with an emphatic declaration that all Christians share in the same Spirit. It is one and the same Spirit who has enabled us all to say "Jesus is Lord" (verses 1–3). It is one and the same Spirit who has distributed to us different gifts (verses 4–11). And it is one and the same Spirit of whom we have drunk and with whom we have been baptized into one Body (verses 12, 13). Nevertheless, this one Body does not consist of one member but of many (verse 14), and he goes on to list some of the different spiritual gifts for service which the one Spirit has bestowed or (for it comes to the same thing) some of the different kinds of Christian work the one Spirit has "appointed" (verse 28).

WHY NOT??

Some of these gifts or workers certainly do not exist in the Church today, notably apostles and prophets, the first two named. Probably some others like "workers of miracles" have also ceased. But we can all agree that "teachers" are still equipped with a teaching gift and appointed to serve in the Church. In Ephesians 4:11 they are linked with "pastors," a word seeming to indicate the more settled pastoral ministry of the Church, and, as in the other passages already quoted, it is only "some" who are appointed to serve in this way and given by Christ to his Church.

DISPENSATIONAL

It is clear, therefore, that although the Body is one to which we all belong, and although the Spirit is one of whom we have all partaken, so that we enjoy a common status and privilege, yet different members of the one Body are appointed and equipped by the one Spirit to perform different functions. Some are "pastors and teachers," or "shepherds and teachers," whose particular calling is to tend and teach the rest of the Flock. So the question before us now is: what is the relation between these two groups, between teachers and taught, shepherds and Flock, or in modern, unbiblical terminology between "clergy" and "laity"? Four main answers have been given to this question. The first is "clericalism."

CLERICALISM

By "clericalism," to which I have already referred, is meant the clerical domination of the laity. That this has been the commonest tendency appears from the fate suffered by the word "lay." Originally, the Greek word *laos* meant quite simply "people," any people or crowd of people. In secular Greek it was used of the population of a city-state, and in biblical Greek of the people of God, first "Israel" in contrast to the Gentiles[6] and then "the new Israel" (the Church) including Gentiles.[7] Thus it was an inclusive word and indicated all the members of a certain people. However, the word had within it from the beginning the seeds of its own decay, for it was natural to continue using it of the masses even when it was desired to distinguish them from their leaders. The *laos* of a Greek city-state were thus distinguished from the *kleros*, the magistrate, and in the Gospels we read of "the chief priests and the rulers and the people,"[8] suggesting that the former were not part of the latter.

In the course of time the English word became even further debased, until in current parlance "lay" is often a synonym for "amateur" as opposed to "professional," or "unqualified" as opposed to "expert." Indeed, the term has developed a largely apologetic flavor when used of oneself ("I'm afraid I'm a layman in this field") and a derisory one when used of others ("he's only a layman, he doesn't speak with knowledge"). Hendrik Kraemer points out that a similar fate has befallen the Greek term *idiotes*, which originally meant the private individual or civilian as opposed to the official, or the ordinary person in contrast to the specialist. This is what the Sanhedrin perceived Peter and John to be, both "uneducated" (*agrammatoi*) and "common men" (*idiotai*).[9] But today, of course, the idiot is not the uncultured person, but the imbecile.

The devaluation of the word "lay" is but a symptom of the devaluation of the people, "laity." Several historical factors contributed to the process. Theologically, the identification of the Christian presbyter with the Old Testament priest and the representation of the Eucharist as the Christian sacrifice, first clearly enunciated by Cyprian, bishop of Carthage, in the middle of the third century, carried with it the priest-people distinction which had existed indeed in the Old Testament. But this has been superseded in the New by the priesthood of all believers, that is, the priesthood of the whole Church. Practically, one suspects that disciplinary problems were a major cause of clericalism, since authoritarian measures were sometimes taken to subdue insubordinate laity. But the Christian presbyter is no more a New Testament apostle than he is an Old Testament priest, and the exercise of ecclesiastical discipline belongs to the whole congregation, not to its leaders only. See, for example, our Lord's injunction, "tell it to the church,"[10] and the apostle's instructions to the Corinthian Church to take action as a body to excommunicate the incestuous offender: "When you are assembled . . . you are to deliver this man to Satan. . . ." And again, "Drive out the wicked person from among you."[11]

However the suppression of the laity arose historically, there can be no doubt that clericalism still permeates much of our thinking today. Kraemer quotes the Roman Catholic author Yves Congar: "Lay people will always form a subordinate order in the church."[12] And though the Church of England has never articulated the matter in such terms, it has often behaved as if it thought this way. Indeed, nearly everybody in England does think this way. People's unconscious identification of the Church with the clergy betrays itself in several popular expressions: "he's going into the Church" for "he is entering the ordained ministry," and "why doesn't the Church do something?" for "why doesn't the archbishop or the episcopate or synod do something?"

Indeed, since I am myself a pastor, I am obliged to ask which of us in the ordained ministry is entirely free from blame. It is true that some of the laity acquiesce too readily in our clericalism. That is to say, they plead that they have no time, or that they are untrained and prefer to leave things to the expert, or that they bear heavy responsibilities in the world and would prefer to be passive and docile and occupy a back seat in the church. And with such pleas they hand over to the clergy obligations and privileges which are theirs by divine right as Christian people. In the words of Sir John Lawrence, "What does the layman really want? He wants a building which looks like a church; a clergyman dressed in the way he approves; services of the kind he's been used to, *and to be left alone.*"[13]

So we clergy trade on their excuses and claim as our prerogative what belongs properly to the whole Church. Thank God some of the more biblically oriented laity revolt. "Too often our pastors seem to treat us only as fund raisers, or cooks, or mimeograph machine operators . . . when our hearts are crying out for a meaningful ministry."[14] Sir Kenneth Grubb records what happened a century ago when Roman Catholic laity in England "showed signs of being uppish." "They were well and truly sat on," he writes.

Mgr George Talbot wrote as follows to Archbishop Manning in 1857, "What is the province of the laity? To hunt, to shoot, to entertain. These matters they understand, but to meddle with ecclesiastical matters, they have no right at all!"[15]

The clerical mind not infrequently goes beyond this kind of condescension to actual tyranny. It manifests itself particularly in the composing of agendas and the chairing of meetings. It is perfectly possible to argue, and it is often argued, that certain subjects (like the conduct of public worship) are the clergyman's prerogative and have nothing to do with the laity. No doubt some church councils and committees contain both unconverted and unspiritual members whose minds are not "governed with the Spirit and Word of God"[16] and who therefore cannot be trusted to decide matters of great spiritual moment for the good of the local church. In some situations a council may need to win its chairman's trust by demonstrating its good sense and spirituality. But when God has blessed a pastor's ministry, and the elected council are mature, responsible Christian men and women, and when a relationship of mutual respect and confidence has developed between minister and council, is there *any* matter affecting the life, worship, work, and witness of the church which should be excluded from its agenda?[17] I can only speak from my own experience that our annual day conferences, in which our priorities as a church have been discussed, including our public worship of God, our fellowship with one another and the church's whole evangelistic program, have proved times of considerable profit and consequent advance.

Further, once items are put on the agenda, the pastor is bound to follow democratic procedures in the conduct of the council's business. His duty is to help the council to discover and clarify its common mind. The very idea of bulldozing the council into letting him have his own way or even of attempting to exercise a chairman's veto should be abhorrent to him. Our own council believes strongly in the Holy Spirit, and in his desire and ability to lead us in any matter to a common mind, the mind of Christ. We have therefore hardly, if ever, taken a vote. To foreclose an issue by a majority decision is usually a sign of impatient unbelief in the Holy Spirit; it can also sow seeds of further discord in the future. Of course several times a difference of opinion has arisen, but our policy has been to go on talking and praying together until we reach agreement rather than to act precipitately and force a division. I can think of two particular issues on which there was a sharp disagreement. The first concerned whether in St. Peter's Church, Vere Street, our beautiful Georgian Chapel of Ease, we should rebuild the old pipe organ or install an electronic one. The second involved the use of modern English in public worship, especially whether God should be addressed as "you." Strong opinions were held on both sides. Opposing views were expressed and argued. The debate for many months was keen. For a while we wondered if we would ever reach agreement and whether it would not be essential to decide by voting. But we sought to be patient, to listen to one another, and understand one another's concerns, and to pray, and in the end the decisions made were, I think, unanimous.

I confess, however, that I personally do not always find these slow, democratic, Christian processes congenial. When an issue becomes tangled, one is tempted to lose patience and cut the Gordian knot. But autocratic clericalism is destructive of the Church, defiant to the Holy Spirit and disobedient to Christ. Christ's own teaching on the subject is unmistakable:

"You know that those who are supposed to rule over the Gentiles lord it over them, and their great men exercise authority over them. But it shall not be so among you; but whoever would be great among you must be your servant (*diakonos*), and whoever would be first among you must be slave (*doulos*) of all."[18]

The contrast is complete. Heathen leadership is characterized by lordship and authority, Christian leadership by service, even slavery. As Hendrik Kraemer neatly puts it, "The lust for power and dominion is exchanged for lust for *diakonia.*"[19] And in this as in all things Jesus is our perfect model. He "emptied himself, taking the form of a servant (*doulos*)."[20] Though his disciples' lord (*kurios*) and teacher, he put on a servant's apron and performed a servant's job in washing their feet.[21] Indeed, he said to them in the same upper room, "I am among you as one who serves" (*ho diakonon*).[22] He added: "If I then, your Lord and Teacher, have washed your feet, you also ought to wash one another's feet. For I have given you an example, that you also should do as I have done to you."[23] As Michael Green has expressed it in his forthright book *Called to Serve:* "Jesus is *the* Servant. . . . The Church must be the Church of the Servant."[24]

The choice between lordship and servitude still confronts every man called to the ministry of the Church. The apostles themselves were conscious of it. "Not that we lord it over your faith," wrote Paul; "we work with you for your joy." "Not as domineering over those in your charge," wrote Peter, "but being examples to the flock."[25] Not lords but servants, not bosses, but fellow workers and examples.

ANTICLERICALISM

The second possible relation between clergy and laity is the exact opposite of the one we have so far been considering. I called the first "clericalism"; I will call the second "anticlericalism." The spirit of clericalism is to despise the laity, and behave as if they did not exist. The spirit of anticlericalism is to despise the clergy and to behave as if they did not exist, or rather, since they do exist, to wish they didn't.

Anticlericalism is a natural and understandably vigorous reaction to clericalism. Historically, it was current clerical abuses which led both Quakers and Christian Brethren to dispense with an ordained ministry altogether, although both preserve some kind of "oversight," corporately exercised over the local meeting or assembly by its acknowledged leaders.

Before going any further, it is important for us to notice that there are traces of a real anticlericalism in the New Testament itself, not because the church leaders were abusing their authority, but because their followers were exhibiting an altogether exaggerated deference toward them. It is this unseemly personality cult which lies behind the slogans recorded in 1 Corinthians 1:12, "I am of Paul, and I of Apollos." Paul is so horrified by this exhibition of allegiance to men instead of to Christ, as if Paul were their crucified Saviour and they had been baptized into the name of Paul, that he cries out with indignant sarcasm: *"What* then is Apollos? *What* is Paul?"[26] He uses the neuter, "what," deliberately, as if he is asking: "What on earth do you suppose we are that you pay this ridiculous homage to us?" And then he answers his own question, almost denigrating his office: We're just *diakonoi,* he says, waiters at table, whom God has been pleased to use. Again, we are nothing but Christ's "underlings" and the stewards of God's revelation,[27] and *that's* how people should regard us.

In this latter half of the twentieth century a new form of anticlericalism is abroad. It is a reaction not to abuse but to redundancy. Since the process of urbanization has (in city areas) made the parochial system (to say the least) artificial, the welfare state has taken over much of the community care previously exercised by clergy, and the distressed often turn for help to a psychiatrist rather than a pastor. Many people are wondering what clergy are now for and whether they are needed any longer. One might call this rather a spirit of aclericalism than of anticlericalism. It must be honestly faced. Is there any room left for clergy? Might not the laity take over?

If we seek an answer to these questions in the right place, namely in the New Testament, I think we must conclude that a pastoral ministry of some kind is part of Christ's permanent purpose for his Church (although it may take different forms—stipendiary and voluntary, full-time and part-time, settled and itinerant), and that we have no authority to abolish it.

Whatever view we may hold of the status of the apostles and the question of their successors, it is clear that the Twelve were appointed by Jesus himself and trained for a special ministry. It is also clear that the Twelve arranged for the appointment of the seven to relieve them of social administration and free them to concentrate on prayer and preaching. Both these groups, however, were in some respects unique. It is when we come to the missionary journeys of Paul that a regular pattern begins to emerge. It is extremely significant that, on revisiting the Galatian cities of Lystra, Iconium, and Antioch, Paul and Barnabas "appointed elders for them in every church, with prayer and fasting."[28] This became Paul's consistent practice. There is no mention in the Acts record of the appointment of elders (presbyter-bishops) in Philippi, but Paul refers to them and to the deacons in his Philippian letter.[29] Again, Luke does not mention in Acts the appointment of elders in Ephesus, but Paul sends for them to Miletus and addresses to them the memorable speech recorded in Acts 20. And when we reach the Pastoral Epistles the same pattern is being continued. "This is why I left you in Crete," Paul writes to Titus, "that you might amend what was defective, and appoint elders in every town as I directed you."[30] Indeed, whatever arrangements were made on the human level for the selection, appointment, and ordination of the pastors of Christ's Flock, the apostle declares that fundamentally they are Christ's gift to his Church.[31]

We must go further than this and say that the elders occupied a real position of leadership in the local church. Two principal verbs are used to denote the character of this leadership. The first is *proïstemi*. "We beseech you, brethren, to respect those who labor among you and *are over you* in the Lord and admonish you, and to esteem them very highly in love because of their work."[32] In 1 Timothy 3:5 it is asked how a man who "does not know how to manage his own household" can possibly "care for God's church." Here *proïstemi* is used for the man's management of his own family, but is changed when it comes to the care of God's. In 1 Timothy 5:17, however, certain elders are specified as being "worthy of double honor," namely those "who rule well," where the verb is *proïstemi* again.

According to the Arndt-Gingrich Lexicon *proïstemi* has two meanings, first to "be at the head of, rule, direct" and secondly to "be concerned about, care for, give aid." It is undoubtedly used in this latter sense in Romans 12:8 ("he who gives aid") and in a similiar way in Titus 3:8, 14, of people who "apply themselves to" or "busy themselves with" good works. But it seems to describe "headship" or "oversight" in reference to the potential presbyters' and deacons' management of their households.[33] Probably, therefore, a similar authority, but over God's household, is intended in both 1 Thessalonians 5:12 and 1 Timothy 5:17. We must observe, however, that the elder's leadership is exercised by "laboring" among the people, and that this "labor" is specified in 1 Timothy 5:17 as being "in preaching and teaching."[34]

The second verb used for clerical leadership is *hegeomai*. It occurs three times in Hebrews 13, translated "your leaders."[35] The same word is used of Joseph when he was *"governor* over Egypt and over all his (Pharaoh's) household"[36] and even of Christ in the quotation from Micah's prophecy: "from you (*sc.* Bethlehem) shall come *a ruler* who will govern (*literally*, 'shepherd') my people Israel."[37] Since this is the word used in Hebrews 13 of local Christian leaders, presumably presbyters, we cannot deny that the minister exercises some kind of "rule." But we must be very careful how we understand it. Luke put the word into the mouth of Jesus himself when he said: "Let the greatest among you become as the youngest, and the leader as one who serves."[38] So then, although Jesus recognizes that there will and must be "leadership" in the Christian Church, he interprets it in terms of service, and the context of Hebrews 13 shows what form this leadership service will take. Christian leaders are to be given both "obedience" and "submission," the author writes, "for they are keeping watch over your souls, as men who will have to give account."[39] Again, it is they who "spoke to you the word of God," whose faith is to be imitated.[40]

Summarizing this evidence, no biblical Christian can give in to the extreme anticlericalism which wants either to dispense with a ministry altogether or deny it any authority. No. Christ and his apostles intended the Church to have a pastoral eldership or "oversight."[41] Such oversight involves some kind of "direction" or "rule." But it is to be seen as a form of service and is to be exercised in general through watching over men's souls and in particular through the teaching of God's Word and through example. We must beware of the spirit of Diotrephes who liked to put himself first.[42] We are called to oversight not lordship, to a leadership which leads not by coercion but by the authority of instruction and example.

DUALISM

If we avoid the extremes of clericalism and of anticlericalism, of a domineering ministry on the one hand and a dispensable one on the other, does this suggest that we should settle for a dualistic compromise? That is, are we to hold that clergy and laity have both received a divine vocation, though a different one, that each party has its own sphere, that we must delineate their territories carefully and avoid all trespass? This is the third possible relation between clergy and laity.

I think it is still the Roman Catholic view. It probably began with the Old Testament analogy of the distinction between priest and people in which the people were forbidden to enter the temple or to sacrifice, while various practices were forbidden to the priests because they had been consecrated to the Lord. However the distinction arose, it is certain that the spread of monasticism hardened it, with its disastrous severance of the sacred from the secular, the Church from the world. "Duo sunt genera Christianorum," wrote Gratian, the twelfth-century lawyer. "There are two sorts of Christians." And Canon Law of the Church of Rome went into elaborate details to define and distinguish the *status clericalis* and the *status laïcalis.*

In *The Documents of Vatican II* there is certainly a welcome new emphasis on the importance of the laity. Introducing the Decree on the Apostolate of the Laity, Martin H. Work quotes the pungent comment of one layman:

> The lay apostolate has been simmering on the "back burner" of the Church's apostolic life for nearly two thousand years, and finally the Fathers of this Council moved it up to the "front burner" and turned the heat up all the way.

Martin Work adds how "everyone hopes it will 'come to a boil' soon. . . ."[43] In the first major document of the Council, *Lumen Gentium,* the Dogmatic Constitution on the Church, clear statements of the equal dignity of clergy and laity appear. For example "all (in the Church) share a true equality with regard to the dignity and to the activity common to all the faithful for the building up of the Body of Christ."[44] Again, "let sacred pastors recognize and promote the dignity as well as the responsibility of the layman in the Church."[45] These are heartening sentiments.

Yet in the same document there are prominent traces of the

older view. In *Mystici Corporis Christi,* the papal encyclical of 1943, it had been stated that bishops are the "primary and principal" element in the constitution of the Church. And Vatican II endorsed this: "In the bishops ... our Lord Jesus Christ ... is present in the midst of those who believe."[46] So apparently it is still by *bishops* that the Church is constituted and the presence of Christ mediated. The order of the early chapters of the Dogmatic Constitution on the Church is significant in this respect. The opening two chapters are entitled "The Mystery of the Church" and "the People of God." But then comes "The Hierarchical Structure of the Church, with special reference to the Episcopate," while "The Laity" is treated separately in chapter 4. This chapter begins: "Having set forth the functions of the hierarchy, this holy Synod gladly turns its attention to the status of those faithful called the laity."[47] They are evidently still second-class citizens after all. They do not themselves constitute the Church; it is just that "their sacred pastors know how much the laity contribute to the welfare of the entire Church."[48] The verbs to "constitute" (of bishops and their assistants, the priests) and to "contribute" (of laity) are revealing of the old dualism.

The Orthodox view is similar to the Roman, but less dualistic. Hendrik Kraemer expresses it by the quotation "clergy and laity make together the fullness (*pleroma*) of the church."[49] However, in contrast to the Church of Rome, the Eastern Orthodox Churches have "a far livelier, more immediate awareness of the wholeness of the Church as the redeemed community in which all are active participants."[50]

What about the Church of England? By contrast with Vatican II's Dogmatic Constitution on the Church mentioned above, it is very welcome to see the Lambeth 1968's Report on "Renewal in Ministry" adopts the opposite order. It begins with "Laymen and Laywomen," continues with the ordained ministry and ends with the episcopate. Yet in the Church of England I would say that a fairly rigid dualism, although not always theologically defined, is nevertheless generally accepted. The parson has his job and the layman his. They are different and should be kept apart. Neither should invade the other's domain. This is a kind of comity arrangement, and comity can easily degenerate into rivalry. At its worst it breeds a "hands off my preserve" attitude, especially in the mind of the clergyman—a mentality which assigns to the laity a lesser and lower role and is therefore but a thinly disguised version of the clericalism we have rejected. At its best, a real partnership can develop, which is infinitely better than either clericalism or anticlericalism, in which parson and people respect each other's dominions and co-exist in happy harmony. It is for "partnership" that George Goyder makes his impassioned plea in his book, *The People's Church.*

But we still have to investigate this dualism and ask where its ground and justification are to be found. It cannot be defended from the New Testament. *Kleros* and *laos* were distinguished as magistrate and people in the Greek city-states, but in the New Testament "they denote the same people, not different people."[51]

Again, we must insist that the distinction between priests and people, so familiar in the Old Testament, each group with its own duties and rights, is not perpetuated in the New. The word *hiereus* is employed in the New Testament only of three people—of Old Testament priests, of Jesus Christ "a great priest over the house of God,"[52] who sacrificed himself once on the cross and ever lives to intercede for us, and of all Christian people whom Christ has made "priests to his God and Father"[53] and who together constitute the priesthood which continuously offers up the spiritual sacrifices of praise and thanksgiving, acceptable to God through Jesus Christ.[54] It is indeed a well-known fact that the word is never used of the Christian minister, who is a presbyter but not a priest.

So we must ask: if the New Testament does not distinguish between *kleros* and *laos,* or between priest and people, but only between the congregation and its leaders, what function is there which a minister may perform and a layman may not? After all, in the Church of England a layman may lead services of worship, and preach if he becomes a licensed Reader. And any layman may baptize in an emergency, so that the validity of baptism does not depend on the baptizer. A lay Reader may also administer the cup at Holy Communion, with special permission. What *biblical* reason can be adduced for allowing him to administer in one kind but not in the other? H. Kraemer describes what happened to the Evangelical (that is the Lutheran) Church in Silesia, 198 of whose 200 pastors were evacuated when Silesia became Polish.

> The laymen took over the care of the Church completely. The Sunday services, including preaching, the administration of the Sacraments, religious instruction for adults and young people, pastoral care in all its forms, were looked after by the laity.[55]

And why not?[56] In that emergency, it was the only solution. We must therefore challenge the dualism which explains the relations between clergy and laity in terms of departmentalization. *Of course* we should largely restrict the administration of Word and Sacraments to the clergy. As Article XXIII puts it: "It is not lawful for any man to take upon him the office of public preaching, or ministering the sacraments in the congregation, before he be lawfully called, and sent to execute the same."[57] But we must be clear that this is a question of *order* not of *doctrine*. It does not in itself supply a satisfactory biblical basis for clergy-laity relations.

SERVICE

Clergy are not to domineer over the laity (clericalism), nor to denigrate themselves and pretend they are altogether dispensable (anticlericalism), or jealously to defend their preserves against trespass, while allocating other preserves to the laity (dualism), but to recognize that the laity are the Church and that they, the clergy, are appointed to serve them, to seek to equip them to be what God intends them to be. This is the fourth and the proper relation between clergy and laity.

We have already seen that we are called to serve, not to rule. We are servants of Christ, his "underlings" or "errand-boys."[58] We are also the servants of others for Christ's sake.[59] And though this is true of every disciple of Christ, it is especially true of those called to positions of leadership in the Church: "Let ... the leader (become) as one who serves."[60] At the beginning of June 1967 the Bishop of Winchester told his Diocesan Conference of a saying current in the Roman Catholic Church since the Second Vatican Council: "The bishops are the servants of the clergy, the clergy are the servants of the laity, the laity are kings with a servant problem." It would not be difficult thus to caricature the call of clergy to serve the laity; we must try to understand how God means it to work out.

The apostle Peter in his first letter takes from Exodus 19:4-6 the epithets with which God through Moses designated the Israelite people, and transfers them to the new Israel, the Christian Church. By so doing he indicates not only who God's people are but what their chief duties and functions are. First, they are "a holy priesthood, to offer spiritual sacrifices acceptable to God through Jesus Christ." It is often said nowadays that the Church exists for the world. This is an unbalanced half-truth. First and foremost the Church exists for God. He has called them out of the world to be his special people,[61] "a people for his name,"[62] that they may give to him the glory which is due to his name. So the first duty of the Church is worship, and the first service of the clergy to the laity should be to help them to worship, to teach them how to worship, to lead them in their worship (though not invariably).

Secondly, Peter wrote:

You are a chosen race, a royal priesthood, a holy nation, God's own people, that you may declare the wonderful deeds of him who called you out of darkness into his marvelous light.[63]

If the Church's first duty is Godward (worship), its second is manward (witness). More generally, the Church is called to ministry. It is a body with many limbs and organs, and each has a service to perform. "There are varieties of service, but the same Lord."[64] This service is *diakonia,* "ministry." So Christian ministry is not and cannot be restricted to the ordained ministry. Kenneth Chafin quotes Francis O. Ayres in *The Ministry of the Laity* (Westminster, 1962):

If you are a baptized Christian, you are already a minister. Whether you are ordained or not is immaterial. No matter how you react, the statement remains true. You may be surprised, alarmed, pleased, antagonized, suspicious, acquiescent, scornful or enraged. Nevertheless, you are a minister of Christ.[65]

And the greatest ministry to which the laity are called is witness to Jesus Christ, evangelism, which means spreading the good news about him. Indeed, in many respects the laity are in a position to engage in this work far more effectively than the clergy, because "the laity is the dispersion of the church,"[66] "immersed in the world,"[67] penetrating more deeply into secular society than the average clergyman will ever get. So it is the clergy's job, so far as we are able, "to minister to the laity as a whole in such a way that it can fulfill its destiny and live as *a Christian laity* in the world of today."[68] Or, in Sir Kenneth Grubb's words,

The layman's job is to be a pioneer. . . . The layman, by the mere fact of living in the world, at his job, in his suburb, on travels for his firm, in his union, at his club, is in a pioneer role. . . . As a pioneer in the world the layman can do much to interpret to the clergyman what it is all about.[69]

And, one might add, as a pastor, the clergyman is to help lay people to live for Christ and witness to Christ in their secular situation. Some suggestions how we may do this I shall reserve for the next chapter.

At this stage what we need to clarify is this relation of clergy to laity, the clergy serving, or one might even say "servicing," the laity. Clear biblical warrant for this privileged relationship is supplied by Ephesians 4:11-12:

> And his gifts were that some should be apostles, some prophets, some evangelists, some pastors and teachers, for the equipment of the saints, for the work of ministry, for building up the body of Christ.

If we erase the comma after the words "saints" and punctuate these verses as Armitage Robinson and others have argued, followed by NEB, we learn why Christ "gave gifts to men," blessing his Church with pastors and teachers. The ultimate reason was "for building up the body of Christ." But how is this to be achieved? Only when pastors and teachers fulfill their calling, which is to "equip the saints for the work of ministry." The "saints" are the laity, all the people of God. Their calling is to engage in "the work of ministry," serving people in the world for Christ's sake. And the calling of the clergy is to "equip" the saints to do it.

How the clergy are to perform this equipping work is suggested in the combination "pastors and teachers." Christian ministers are pastors, shepherds of Christ's flock. This is their only essential distinctness. Of course they are themselves also Christ's sheep. But they are called to be shepherds. The Church is a universal priesthood and also a universal diaconate, for all God's people are called to *diakonia*. But the Church is not a universal pastorate. All God's people are priests; all are ministers or servants; but "he gave *some* . . . pastors and teachers."

The chief function of the pastor is teaching, for the chief duty of the shepherd is to feed or pasture his sheep. The ordained ministry is fundamentally a teaching ministry. This is why the ordination candidate must be "apt to teach"[70] and must also "hold firm to the sure word as taught, so that he may be able to give instruction in sound doctrine and also to confute those who contradict it."[71]

But, it may be objected, if the relation between clergy and laity is that of shepherd to sheep, of the teacher to the taught, are we not back where we started? Are we not guilty of encouraging lay passivity, even inertia (the clergy being the leaders) and lay ignorance (the clergy being the teachers)? Certainly there is an element here we cannot escape. At the same time, we repudiate both lordship and paternalism. And if it be said that the pastoral relationship makes the clergyman a subject and the layman an object, we must immediately add that it is only in order to help the layman to become himself a subject. The great purpose of the teaching ministry is not to tie our pupils to our apron-strings, but rather to help to lead them into spiritual maturity and active ministry.

There must be many of us in the Church, both clergy and laity, who need to perform a complete mental somersault. It is not the clergyman who is the really important person and the lay person a rather inferior brand of churchman, but the other way round. It is the laity who are important, the whole Church serving both God and man, the vanguard of Christ's army as it advances to the conquest of the world, and the clergy are the servicing organization.[72]

We must once for all give up defining the laity in relation to and in distinction from the clergy. Yet this is the usual procedure. Who are the laity? The *Oxford Dictionary* answer is "the body of the people not in orders, as opposed to the clergy." The *Oxford Dictionary of the Christian Church* is no better. It defines "Laity" as "Members of the Christian Churches who do not belong to the clergy." Dr. Kathleen Bliss expresses a trenchant criticism of all such negative attitudes to and definitions of the laity.

Clergy / Laity

For these, she writes, "have in them a strong element of 'over-againstness' toward the clergy—the clergy are, and the laity are not; the clergy do, and the laity must not. Nobody wants to be an 'is not'. . . ."[73] Instead, we must start defining the clergy in relation to the laity. The laity are the whole people of God, purchased by his precious blood, and some of us are given the great privilege of their oversight, shepherding and serving them for Christ's sake. The common phrase "clergy and laity" is essentially dualistic. Clergy are not hyphenated to the laity as if they were a separate class; they are "ministers *of* the people" because they themselves belong to the people they are called to serve.

I cannot conclude this chapter better than with something Paul wrote to the Corinthians. They were saying "I belong to Paul," "I belong to Apollos," or "I belong to Cephas." In other words, they were defining themselves in relation to their leaders. Paul told them that the opposite was the truth. "All things are yours, whether Paul or Apollos or Cephas . . . all are yours."[74] So if anybody belongs to anybody in the Church, it is not the laity who belong to the clergy, but the clergy who belong to the laity. We are theirs, their servants for Jesus' sake. In olden days it was customary for a lay person to conclude a letter to his bishop with the words, "I have the honor to be, sir, your obedient servant." It would be more biblical, however, for a bishop (or any pastor) to sign himself a lay person's obedient servant!

3

The Christian Testimony

(*marturia*)

In the last chapter I suggested that the whole Church is in a sense a "diaconate" because it is called to *diakonia,* to service. "I am among you as one who serves," Jesus said,[1] and gave a visual demonstration of his words by girding himself with a servant's apron and washing his disciples' feet. Then, when he had resumed his place at supper, he said to them:

> If I . . . your Lord and Teacher, have washed your feet, you also ought to wash one another's feet. For I have given you an example, that you also should do as I have done to you. Truly, truly, I say to you, a servant is not greater than his master.[2]

So every Christian is called to service. — NOT OPTIONAL

But *diakonia* is a general word; there are many forms of service. As Dr. Gustaf Wingren, Professor of Systematic Theology at the University of Lund in Sweden, has written in his theological study of preaching and the Church:

> Ordination of a Lutheran priest implies that in a Church where all are essentially priests, a household of God, he receives the special

task of preaching the Word and dispensing the sacraments. The particular office which the priest holds is for Lutheranism but a special case of a general sharing out of vocations. The ministry of the priest is no *more* a ministry than is that of the mother or the doctor; it is simply that he has a *different* ministry from theirs, a totally different. . . . The word "ministry" is a word without content until it is known *what* ministry is in mind. Indeed, the practice of going around talking about "the ministry" as something definite is an objectionable usage for a Lutheran priesthood, and implies in itself a false cleavage between the congregation and the priest, however modestly it may be done.[3]

Acts 6 supplies a good example of the varied usage of *diakonia* in the New Testament. We are familiar with the appointment of the seven by the twelve. The apostles said "it is not right that we should give up preaching the word of God to serve tables" (verse 2). But it is important to notice that both "the ministry of the word" (verse 4) and the serving of tables (verse 2) are alluded to as forms of *diakonia.* Some would no doubt regard the one ministry as spiritual and the other as social, but both were "service" and both required spiritual men to perform it.

The opportunities for *diakonia,* for a ministry in which Christian people may serve both God and man, are extremely numerous. There is the vocation of parents to bring up their children "in the discipline and instruction of the Lord"[4] and to make the Christian home a place of love, hospitality, and peace. There is a Christian's job, to be regarded primarily neither as a way to earn his living nor as a contribution to his country's economic stability, nor as a useful sphere of witness and evangelism—not in fact as a means to these or any other estimable ends—but as an end in itself, the *diakonia* of a Christian man, who is seeking to cooperate with the purpose of God in securing the welfare of men. There are also abundant openings for alert Christians in public service, through voluntary organizations, and among underprivileged and unwanted people in the neighborhood.

But apart from the home, the job and the neighborhood, most Christians will wish to be of service also in and through the local church to which they belong. It is fashionable nowadays, at least among more radical writers, to deride the notion of "church service" as a regrettable kind of ecclesiastical self-centeredness and to insist that the proper sphere of a Christian's service is not the Church but the world. I do not deny the truth contained in this assertion. No Christian should live out his entire spare-time life in the sheltered seclusion of the church; he has been sent by his Master into the world, there to serve others humbly in his name. Yet we must not become unbalanced in applying this principle, either by denying that some church service is rightly church-centered or by asserting that it is all of this kind. Let me enlarge on these two points.

First, if a local church is to fulfill its God-given obligations of worship and fellowship, innumerable practical tasks have to be done. They are usually and rightly shared out among church members. I have in mind such good works as flower arrangement, clerical assistance, hospitality and catering, cleaning the church, mending the books, repairing the robes, and maintaining the building and its furnishings. To these essential jobs we have ourselves in London added a nursery for babies on Sunday mornings, the entertainment of visitors to lunch or coffee after Sunday services, and church guides who show visitors around on Sunday afternoons. These tasks are good and necessary; they should not be despised.

In the second place, however, it is a mistake to imagine that "church service" is limited to this kind of church-centered activity. The service of the local church should include its evangelistic outreach to the parish or district in which the church building is situated. Each worshiping community should be a witnessing community as well, and should be witnessing in the very neighborhood in which it gathers for worship. There is something very anomalous about a congregation which claims to be worshiping God, yet ignores the local residents who do not worship him also.

So one of the major aspects of true "church service" will be the church's witness in its own district. Such service is not church-centered, since its concern is the secular world outside, but it will be church-based. The church is not the sphere in which it is performed, but the base of operations from which it is carried out.

This second aspect of church service also has many sections, which I will describe later, but they all have this in common: they all involve the opening of the mouth in *marturia,* in spoken testimony to people. For the Christian Church is a testifying Church, and every Christian is called to be a witness. Possibly the last words which fell from the lips of the risen Christ before his ascension contained his command to be witnesses and his promise of the coming Spirit:

> You shall receive power when the Holy Spirit has come upon you; and you shall be my witnesses in Jerusalem and in all Judea and Samaria and to the end of the earth.[5]

We have no authority to separate the promise and the command from each other. If the gift of the Spirit belongs to all believers, the duty of witness belongs to all believers also.

Further, Christians need teaching and training for witness. Some would deny this. But those who do so probably have an unbalanced notion of witness, as if it meant merely the sharing of one's personal experience. The word "witness" is not a synonym for autobiography, however; it means essentially testimony to Christ. "You shall be *my* witnesses," he said. Again, "the Spirit of truth . . . will bear witness *to me;* and you also are witnesses."[6] Although witness to Christ may and should be illustrated and confirmed from our own experience, it is still about Christ that the true witness speaks, rather than about himself. But if he is to speak about Christ, he must know about Christ—not just the Christ of his own experience, but the Christ of the apostolic testimony. For the Christ about whom he must speak is the authentic Christ of the New Testament, whose birth, life, death, resurrection, heavenly reign, and coming glory the apostles set forth in the New Testament documents.

And it is with this teaching and training of the laity to witness, as we began to suggest in the last chapter, that ordained ministers are particularly concerned. The laity have their *diakonia* (service), and especially their *marturia* (witness); the *diakonia* of the clergy is to help them to exercise it. Thus the humblest minister may borrow the customary designation of the Pope and style himself *servus servorum Dei*.

Dr. Elton Trueblood, a prominent American Quaker, has raised the whole question of the purpose and function of the ordained ministry. He knows that many clergy are feeling frustrated and are uncertain of their function. They are sick and tired of appearing to exist merely in order to say an official prayer at functions or grace before banquets, and of being involved in endless promotional activity. As a result, many American clergy are leaving the ministry. Dr. Trueblood says he knows of one insurance company which "now employs more than a hundred former pastors."[7] It is essential, therefore, to discover what a clergyman's distinctive ministry is. Dr. Trueblood describes it as an "equipping ministry." He adds that he borrows the phrase from others,[8] although they in their turn derive the word from the RSV rendering of Ephesians 4:11,12: Christ's "gifts were that some should be ... pastors and teachers, for the *equipment* of the saints, for the work of ministry." Dr. Trueblood goes on to write of the vital importance of training the laity: "To watch for underdeveloped powers, to draw them out, to bring potency to actuality in human lives—this is a self-validating task."[9]

If this work is fundamental to the duties of a clergyman, Dr. Trueblood asks what we should call him. He is certainly a "minister," but so is a layman. To call him an "elder," he suggests, is rather absurd if he is a young man, as is "father" if he is a bachelor. "Preacher" refers to only one aspect of his ministry and "pastor," though true and biblical, is somewhat misleading. "Sheep are not particularly productive, except in providing wool and mutton,"[10] and are also "notorious for their placidity." Besides, many town-dwellers have never even seen a sheep!

So Dr. Trueblood settles for the word "coach."

> Everyone knows that, in the development of a football or a baseball team, the quality of the coaching staff often makes a crucial difference.... The glory of the coach is that of being the discoverer, the developer and the trainer of the powers of other men.... The Christian coach will be one who is more concerned ... in developing others than in enhancing his own prestige.[11]

Keith Miller, the Episcopal layman from Corpus Christi, Texas, who studied under Dr. Trueblood, takes up this theme in *The Taste of New Wine.* He also refers to the clergyman as an "equipping minister" or "resource person," and adds that new church structures "call for a kind of dying of our ecclesiastical ego." No longer can the minister occupy the center of the stage with "God in the wings and the congregation as paying spectators." Rather must the congregation hold the stage, in their homes and communities, with "the minister in the wings and God the author of the drama as the audience." He goes on:

> The parish minister must love Christ enough to die to the centrality of his role in the church. He must become the coach, the teacher and pastor of the laymen who will be the new focus of attention in the developing renewal movement.[12]

If this basic idea is accepted, that the laity are called to *diakonia* and especially *marturia,* and that the distinctive *diakonia* of the clergy is to train them for it, let me illustrate this principle from our experience in London, first regarding the training of the laity and secondly regarding their service.

THE TRAINING OF THE LAITY

Before I come to the details of the lay training scheme which we have tried to develop, I think I need to enforce a little more the necessity of a training program of some kind. I have myself found it helpful to remember that our Lord's own ministry was a balanced one. He divided his time between preaching to the multitudes, counseling individuals and training the twelve. Most clergy are involved in the first two—preaching to the congregation and interviewing individual people; it is the third which we tend to neglect. It is quite true that the training of the apostles was a unique ministry. Yet the principle of giving to a select group of potential leaders a more intensive course of instruction seems still to apply today. I think we may say that a ministry of preaching and counseling, to the exclusion of group training, is an unbalanced ministry, for it does not follow the pattern of Christ.

Certainly the responsibility of the clergy to train the laity has been increasingly recognized in the Anglican Communion. Archbishop Temple is quoted in *Towards the Conversion of England* as saying that "the main duty of the clergy must be to train the lay members of the congregation in their work of witness."[13] Similarly, Archbishop Cyril Garbett wrote in *The Claims of the Church of England:* "no effort should be spared to build up in every parish a band of lay men and women who are not only devoted to their church but who can give an intelligent reason for their membership."[14] In 1954 at Evanston, the Second Assembly of the World Council of Churches made this statement:

> The laity stand at the very outposts of the Kingdom of God. They are the missionaries of Christ in every secular sphere. Theirs is the task to carry the message of the Church into every area of life, to be informed and courageous witnesses to the will of our Lord in the world. To this end they will need training and guidance.[15]

And now Lambeth 1968 has added its own earnest appeal:

> No one wants untrained troops. Anglicans pay lip service to train-
> ing, but in fact it has generally stopped by the age of fifteen. We
> need a Christian education explosion comparable to that in the sec-
> ular world (p. 97).

Hence Resolution 27:

> The Conference believes that there is an urgent need for increase in
> the quantity and quality of training available for lay people for
> their task in the world (p. 38).

But are the laity ready and willing to be trained? Are they not
already overpressed by multitudinous activities? Can we really
expect them to undertake a course of serious training, followed
by responsible service? I believe the answer to these questions is
that if the laity to whom we are referring are truly Christian, that
is, personally committed to Jesus Christ as their Saviour and
Lord, then they are not only ready but eager to serve him, and
that they are disappointed, frustrated and even spiritually
wounded, if we do not help them to fulfill their God-given calling to be active witnesses to Jesus Christ.

We have now held a Training School at All Souls Church
every year since 1950. During this time the average annual number of successful candidates has been nearly 43. This does not
mean (I hasten to add) that the 718 who have so far been commissioned are all still active. The position at the present time is
that only 166 are. The rest have had to resign their commissions,
mostly through leaving London. Many of these are now serving
in other churches, while a number are in the ordained ministry or
on the mission field. But it is interesting that the average number
of years of service given by those still active is about five-and-a-
half, and I learn from the questionnaire recently submitted to
them (which 103 of them completed) that on average they spend

nearly three hours a week on the particular church work which has been assigned to them. All this seems to be clear evidence of the keenness of lay people to be equipped for active service in the Church. "I received great blessing from the Lord when attending the Confirmation Classes," wrote one of them, a Health Visitor, "and then had a great inward desire to serve him in some way." So she enrolled in the Training School and is now engaged in house-to-house visitation.

How, then, are the laity to be trained? In one sense, if the ministry of the Church is faithful, they are being trained all the time. That is to say, one cannot distinguish rigidly between "teaching" and "training," and every pastor's ambition, through the regular ministry of Word and sacrament, through counseling and example, is to "present every man mature in Christ."[16] Nevertheless, for the work of witness in the parish, especially for such tasks as visiting in people's homes and leading Sunday School or Bible study classes, some extra and more specific training is clearly needed.

Our own training program, which has to be undertaken before lay people are eligible to engage in parochial *marturia,* is in three stages, first the Annual Training School itself, secondly the examination, and thirdly the Commissioning Service.

First, the Training School. This consists of a course of twelve lectures on the theory and practice of evangelism, one evening lecture a week from October to February, with a break over Christmas. An explanatory leaflet is printed, which contains an enrollment form. An open invitation is given to members of the congregation to enroll in the school, while at the same time a more personal approach is made to the previous year's confirmation class and to certain individuals whose spiritual gifts and potentiality have been noticed. The lecture course is divided into two equal halves. The first is entitled "the theology of the gospel" and introduces the doctrines of God and man, of Jesus Christ, the cross, the Holy Spirit and the Church. The second section is called "the practice of evangelism" and comprises talks on "how to be fit for the Master's use," "how to persevere when discouraged," "how to lead a friend to Christ," "how to meet common objections," "how to speak for Christ" and "how to visit in homes." Duplicated lecture summaries are supplied, and loose-leaf notebooks to contain these are on sale. Most of those attending also make notes of their own. We think the school is probably a bit too academic and theoretical, and that more opportunity should be given both for discussion on the one hand and practical training on the other (although the latter comes later). However, over 86 percent of those who answered the questionnaire considered the course about right. "How thrilling and satisfying even limited study of the Word of God can be" was the reaction of an elderly lady candidate, while the comment of a middle-aged bank cashier was: "pretty tough going, but don't reduce it."

The next step is the written exam which is taken by candidates in their own home. We make it clear that, although they may use their Bible as much as they like, we trust them not to use their lecture summaries or notes or any other aid. Most people have found the exam quite easy. The first question we ask is basic, such as, "What is the Gospel?" or, "What is a Christian?" to ensure so far as possible that the candidate himself is a sincere believer. Other sample questions in recent years have been: "Write out in full, with the references, any two verses of Scripture which you might use in explaining to an inquirer the steps to Christ," "Summarize *either* the evidence for the diety of Jesus *or* the work of the Holy Spirit." "What are the chief motives for evangelism?" "Give a brief reply to the following remarks: 'Science has disproved the Bible;' 'The Church is full of hypocrites;' 'I'm perfectly happy as I am;' 'I can't reconcile all the suffering of the world with a God of love;' 'I'm just not interested.' "

The written exam is followed by a personal interview which provides an opportunity both for going through the corrected exam paper and for a personal assessment of the candidate. At the same time some discussion takes place about the particular kind of service which each will undertake. This is decided by mutual agreement, in the light of the current needs and the candidate's ability, experience, and preference.

It might be thought that the setting of this combined written and oral examination would constitute an ordeal sufficiently distasteful to put many people off. But we have not found this to be so. Probably we should be more flexible in allowing some people (who are, for example, more elderly or more experienced or less educated) to qualify without the necessity of a written exam. And indeed we already make some exceptions, but the general rule has stood the test of time, and over 95 percent agreed in the questionnaire with the rightness of having one. They see its value in providing an incentive to study and review, in helping to consolidate knowledge and crystallize thought, and in judging the fitness of each candidate for service in the parish.

Next comes the commissioning service, which takes place on a midweek evening, sometimes in church, sometimes more informally in a hall. Our bishop has been kind enough to come each year for it. After a few questions modeled on the ordination services, touching the candidates' fitness, sense of call, and undertaking to be faithful, the bishop uses the following words of commissioning: "May the love of God the Father encompass you. May the presence of God the Son uphold you. May the power of God the Holy Spirit rest upon you. Go forth in the name of God, as the ambassadors of Christ and the servants of men, and may the Lord bless your labors abundantly." Prayers and a blessing conclude the service, after which each receives his commissioning certificate. Some people find the service too formal and impersonal, but most agree that it increases the candidates' sense of the importance and privilege of the service they will do. It has often been a truly solemn occasion. "I really felt I had been commissioned," wrote one person afterwards. It is interesting to read the concern expressed in the Lambeth 1968 Report "at the lack of any form of commissioning for laymen analogous to the ordination of clergy" (p. 99). Resolution 25 recommends an exploration of the theology of baptism and confirmation "in relation to the need to commission the laity for their task in the world" (p. 37).

We do not of course imagine that a fairly elementary course of twelve lectures, even if it is followed by an examination and a commissioning, is an adequate training for all forms of Christian service. But it is at least a basic minimum. It is also supplemented by three or four meetings for all Commissioned Workers each year, in which some further instruction is given and through which a continuing cohesion is given to the work. But more specialized training is attempted for groups like Sunday School teachers, and it seems clear that further advance along this line is needed.

The index of Commissioned Workers is constantly kept up to date. It is generally understood both that certain tasks in the work of the Church are "commissioned service," which may be performed only by those who have been commissioned, and that if a Commissioned Worker gives up his commissioned service (unless he transfers to another branch of it) he must resign his commission.

THE SERVICE OF THE LAITY

We turn now from the training of the laity to the service of the laity. What tasks do Commissioned Workers undertake? They are many and varied. But since they are all forms of *marturia* and involve relationship to *people,* perhaps the best classification is in terms of the people to whom the witness is borne.

The first and largest group is the residents of the parish—nearly 9,000 of them according to the latest census. Since it is the general duty of every church to take the gospel to the people who do not come to hear it, and since it is the particular duty of every Church of England church to care for the souls of the parish, we have always tried to emphasize the importance of house-to-house visitation. Most Commissioned Workers begin their service by doing at least a year of this kind of visiting. The parish has been divided into three geographical areas, each with a district superintendent and a group of visitors. These go out two by two, like the twelve and the seventy, into the homes of the street or block allocated to them. It should be clearly understood that their objective in visiting is not to canvass for money, nor just to make a friendly social call from the church, nor even (at least in the first instance) to invite the people to come to church, but to be witnesses to Jesus Christ. This does not mean that they will be rude or brash or tactless. It may well take them time to win people's confidence before it would be right or wise for them to witness. They may also leave Christian literature and invite those visited to a special guest service or meeting. But they do not forget their primary responsibility, which is themselves to speak of Jesus Christ.

At the time of writing, we have just been giving further thought to the objective of this house-to-house visiting. Have we been right to define it almost exclusively in terms of witness? The Statement of the National Evangelical Anglican Congress (1967) affirmed that "Evangelism and compassionate service belong together in the mission of God."[17] What, then, should be the response of house-to-house visitors to some social need which they discover, such as a marriage breakdown, or unemployment, or a financial crisis, or a defaulting landlord? Should they become involved in such things? Or would this social involvement distract them from their evangelistic task? After full discussion we have been brought to a common mind about this question. House-to-house visitors have always tried to lend a helping hand in situations of social need, but now we have clarified their responsibility. We are bringing into being a new group of Commissioned Workers to be called "Welfare Visitors," to whom a case of social need may be referred, but only in certain circumstances. House-to-house visitors are not merely witnesses. They are also Christians! So because Christians are called to love and by love to serve,[18] and because the visitors enter homes as Christian people, they must keep their eyes open for social as well as spiritual need, and they must have liberty to seek to meet whatever need they find. Only if some situation is likely to demand more time or more specialized knowledge than they have at their disposal are they encouraged to call in a Welfare Visitor.

Door-to-door visiting is arduous and exacting. Tramping the streets and climbing the steep stairs of tenement blocks is tiring after a hard day's work in the office. Many homes are occupied by foreign visitors or immigrants—Cypriot, Chinese, Italian, Pakistani—and the language barrier proves a formidable obstacle. Often the television set is on, and the visitors are made to feel unwelcome. In some cases the reception is worse than cool; it is actively hostile. But perhaps the clearest impression gained by the visitors is the size of the gulf in contemporary England which separates the masses from the Church. "People are self-satisfied and do not want to know of Christ," writes one. There is "deep misunderstanding" of Christian truth, says another, while people's objections are more often based on hearsay than on personal conviction. A third speaks of "the widespread and appalling ignorance of the gospel," which she has discovered in her visiting.

So this visiting is tough. Many visitors have declared that the biggest lessons which they themselves have learned through their commissioned service are the need for "patience and endurance," for "tolerance," for "boldness" or "self-discipline" or "compassion," while others have come to see with limpid clarity that "the conversion of souls is the Holy Spirit's work," and that "unless we go in God's strength we are powerless." Although we have tried to encourage the visitors by periodical Visiting Campaigns, in which members of the church staff join, and by a Parish Survey, in which the use of a questionnaire has opened up many conversations, we still recognize what a difficult labor this visiting is, requiring strong Christian qualities of perseverance and a constant, humble reliance on the Holy Spirit himself.

Yet there have also been a number of encouragements. Several visitors have spoken of "the joy of being able to speak to people about Christ" or "the joy of being able to witness, sometimes spending over an hour with people, being bombarded with questions, and having real peace even when not knowing all the answers!" Others have been surprised by the spiritual receptivity of some people they have visited. When "talking to people about the Lord Jesus Christ," one described "how willing most of them are to listen to us." And some could testify to the thrill of "seeing someone we visited eventually coming to love the Lord."

A second group of people, for whom the Church has a special responsibility, is the elderly and the sick. We have a small group of Health Visitors who attend a monthly Service of Prayer for the Sick and are asked, in particular, to pray for and visit some who are chronically ill. There is a much larger group of "Old People's Welfare Visitors." Instead of going in pairs from door to door like the house-to-house visitors, these Old People's Welfare Visitors go singly and regularly to visit just one or two senior citizens. As a group they too have a superintendent, who is in touch with the local Old People's Welfare Association and the various services for old people provided by the borough. Being called "Old People's *Welfare* Visitors," their concern is for the total welfare of those they visit, spiritual as well as physical and social. The practical tasks they are able to perform are innumerable, ranging from letter-writing, shopping, cooking, and handling pension problems, to the provision of radios, spectacles, dentures, and fracture boards.

This visiting is exacting also. Each visitor has to learn to be a good listener. One speaks of "the joy and the heartache of sharing the ups and downs in the life of the old lady" she visits. One or two are visiting hardened atheists and find it a great trial to persevere in love and friendship toward them. But others can tell of real blessing. "Some of the folk I have visited have become very dear friends," says one. Another writes of "the joy of loving, giving to, sharing with, and serving the old ladies" whom she visits. Another has learned from this visiting that "it is in giving that we truly receive." What do they receive? This is what they say is their reward: "the increasing faith and holiness in some old people," or "seeing Miss W.'s face when she opens the door," while another declares "I feel Mrs C. has a greater desire for spiritual things than I; she exhorts me now!" It is often touching to observe the loving care extended to these old folk, as a result of which seven or more of them are being looked after in a small old people's home which our church opened in the parish seven years ago.

The third group among whom Commissioned Workers are laboring is children and young people. Some are Sunday School teachers, others help with a Sunday morning family service, and others are club leaders in the parochial community center which has been operating since 1958. In it a full range of clubs is provided for all ages, with emphasis on young people. Those who work in the clubhouse (as it is called) are divided into "club leaders" and "club helpers." Club helpers do trojan service in the canteen and the office and in other practical ways, but do not need to be commissioned. Club leaders are all commissioned, however, and exercise a spiritual responsibility in the clubs they lead. They work together as a team, and although they have some disciplinary and other problems, they can also bear witness to a living God who is at work in their midst. One club leader says, "I have found that giving out love has enriched my own life." A Sunday School teacher finds it specially rewarding to see how "small children really understand important truths, for instance when they start to pray themselves instead of just repeating what they have heard from adults," while another club leader has been deeply impressed "to see the teenagers change when they have accepted Christ."

Fourthly, some Commissioned Workers are seeking to serve

the young Christians of the congregation, the babes of God's family, the lambs of Christ's flock. Those who come forward in response to the invitation given at the monthly guest service are all counseled, and every counselor is, of course, a Commissioned Worker. We then invite them into a so-called "Nursery Class." We find the title a trifle embarrassing, but nonetheless we have never succeeded in changing it. At least it has the merit of accuracy since the Nursery Class is designed for newborn babes in Christ, who are still at the nursery stage. Each Nursery Class meets weekly. It is intended to help spiritual babes to take their first simple steps in Bible reading and prayer, and to begin to draw them into the Church's fellowship. There are now seven Nursery Classes, meeting on different days of the week and at different times, and most of the leaders and assistant leaders are lay people and again Commissioned Workers. Perhaps they have the greatest privilege of all in commissioned service, because they are allowed to watch God evidently at work in human lives. One Nursery Class leader describes the wonderful joy of seeing "the miracle of the new birth and growth of the young Christian," while the leader of a Secondary Class (to which many Nursery Class members graduate) mentions the similar joy of "seeing spiritual babes grow to manhood."

Not that every new Christian joins a Nursery Class or that everyone who does stays the course. There are disappointments and discouragements in this branch of service too. One Nursery Class leader has specially learned, she says, that "all efforts to cajole or persuade people to attend are worse than useless if you don't *pray.*"

The fifth group whom Commissioned Workers try to serve I will call "strangers"—strangers to London and especially strangers from overseas. Being a London church, we receive a steady stream of letters from all over the world, from grannies and aunties, parents and cousins, clergy and friends, telling us that someone is arriving in London and asking us if we will make contact with them. To such we want to show that *philoxenia* ("love for strangers" or "hospitality") which is required of Christian people.[19] So we have a small group of Commissioned Workers, called "sponsors" for want of a better name, whose task is to get in touch with a person commended to us, befriend him, invite him to church and/or a midweek activity, introduce him to others, and stand by him until he feels that he really belongs to the fellowship.

The largest number of such "strangers" comes from overseas. These include visitors on vacation, business people, *au pair* girls and especially students. Most of the latter come to take courses in London University (17 percent of whose student body is from overseas) and in other colleges, a significant number of them undertaking some kind of advanced graduate study. In order to help us to care for them we appointed a layman in 1963 as "Counselor to Overseas Visitors." He is responsible for the church's International Fellowship.

A team of Commissioned Workers shares the ministry with him, especially in the leadership of a number of international Bible study groups. On the whole, they find it exciting work. "If we try to do it in our own strength," write a young married couple who are leaders of one such group, "we get flustered and frustrated. We have learned to trust the Lord to help us." When they do use spiritual weapons in spiritual work, they add, they have the joy of "seeing 'shaky' Christians mature and their faith deepen."

The sixth group of people among whom Commissioned Workers labor are ordinary members of the congregation. Large numbers of them belong to small Fellowship Groups, nearly all of which have lay leaders, all of whom, together with their deputy leaders, are Commissioned Workers. I will not delay on their responsibilities now, because the next chapter will be devoted to this subject.

This, then, is an approximate classification of commissioned service. Commissioned Workers are engaged in the systematic visitation of parishioners, the chronic sick and the elderly; in the teaching and training of the young; in the nurture of new Christians; in the care of strangers, and in the pastoral oversight of church members.

AN EVALUATION

Looking back over the seventeen years in which this program of the training, examining, commissioning, and service of the laity has been operating, we are perhaps in a position to make a critical assessment of it. What are its weaknesses, and what are its values?

I think the first weakness has been in the realm of inadequate supervision. Twenty-five of those who answered the questionnaire mentioned this in one way or another. The Sunday School, Clubhouse and International Fellowship workers seem to belong to closely knit and well supervised groups, but some of the visitors, especially the house-to-house visitors who are in the frontline of the church's advance into the parish, feel they need more support, not least from the clergy. I do not believe this is a lingering clericalism which is to be resisted, but rather a genuine desire that lay commissioned service will be in partnership with the work of the clergy and not a substitute for it. I myself have only recently learned that the true art of delegation is not to hand over work to somebody else and then forget about it, but to commit work to a deputy who knows that he is responsible to you and can at times report back and seek advice.

The second weakness, like the first, is a danger to which the scheme is prone, rather than an inevitable and intrinsic weakness. It is, in fact, a danger to which the administration of every kind of spiritual work is exposed. It concerns the relation between form and spirit, between organization and freedom. It is possible that the training-examining-commissioning sequence actually inhibits the free enterprise of those not commissioned, because they may feel they have no liberty to work for Christ if they are not commissioned. In this situation we need to insist strongly that Christian people are perfectly free to fulfill their duties to witness and engage in other forms of Christian activity without waiting to be organized into it by the local church or needing official permission to begin it! The purposes of training and commissioning are to encourage, improve, and coordinate the service of the laity in the local church and parish, not to frustrate it or quench the Spirit.

Turning from the weaknesses and perils of this scheme to its advantages, I think we may say that it has a threefold value.

First, it makes possible genuine teamwork between clergy and laity in *diakonia*. It encourages the laity to bear the witness to which God calls them ("the joy of serving the Lord and making him known to others," as one describes it) and it enables the clergy to fulfill their God-given role in helping to equip them for it.

Secondly, if the scheme encourages some, it also discourages others. And this is necessary. As one of our more senior Commissioned Workers has expressed it, herself holding an Inter-Diocesan Certificate: "it has encouraged many diffident Christians to undertake active service for which they would never have offered themselves . . . and perhaps checked some who would have been too self-assertive." This negative value of the scheme is more important than may at first sight appear. Would it be an exaggeration to say that one of the scandals of the contemporary ecclesiastical scene is the number of unsuitable and uninstructed people who are teaching in the Church's Sunday Schools? I do not think this an overstatement. Many teachers are, of course, well qualified and deeply devoted; but many others are quite unsure of themselves, their faith and their personal relationship to Jesus Christ. Now one good thing which the training and commissioning arrangement has done for us is firmly and finally to close the back door into the privileged service of the Church. If anybody now volunteers to visit or teach or counsel, one can say

"Fine! The Training School begins in October." Surely a responsible church *must* ensure that its accredited visitors, teachers, leaders, and counselors have received at least a modicum of training? They represent Christ and his Church; they need to be equipped for this honorable service. I was relieved and heartened to find in the questionnaire that, in answer to the question, "Do you approve or disapprove of our insistence on training and commissioning before anybody is entrusted with spiritual church work?" 96 percent of those who replied said they approved, the great majority emphatically and wholeheartedly.

The third value of the scheme which is worth a mention concerns the "status" which a Commissioned Worker enjoys. True, all "status" has its perils, and fallen human beings even if born again and baptized into Christ are not exempt from temptations to pride and jealousy. True also, it is quite possible for training to be given and service to be rendered without any episcopal commissioning. Nevertheless, a number of Commissioned Workers have realized the advantages of commissioning. Some acknowledge that their position has helped them to take their work more seriously, to be disciplined in it and to realize their commitment to the service to which they have been assigned. Others have found in their commissioning not so much an incentive for themselves as a certain authority in the eyes of others, especially as a means of entry into people's homes. "It gives me confidence," one has written, "to know that I go as a representative, and with the support, of the Church."

Let me conclude this chapter with a clarification: the particular pattern of Training School and commissioned service which we have developed is certainly no stereotype for every other church—especially those in different situations. It is entirely dispensable. But the training and the service of the laity are not. These are indispensable, at least in any church which seeks to conform its life to New Testament teaching. What matters is the fundamental principle of the laity's *marturia,* and their need of the clergy's *diakonia* in equipping them for it; the precise pattern in which this principle is expressed may vary in every church.

POSTSCRIPT

What you have just read was written in 1968 and published in 1969. The following year Michael Baughen succeeded me as team leader at All Souls Church, and naturally changes began to take place. In 1976 he appointed Andrew Cornes as Director of Training, who at once began to devise a much more comprehensive program than the old Annual Training School. I have watched the developments with great interest, and wholeheartedly approve of them.

The fundamental philosophy remains the same, namely that every member of the Body of Christ is gifted for service, called to service, and needs to be trained for service. It is significant that Andrew has chosen the expression "The Equipment Room" as the umbrella title for all the training schemes now available at All Souls. For the program, he writes, "is not interested in climbing to some high-powered intellectual plane or in cramming people's minds with irrelevant facts." Instead, "its one aim is to equip Christians with the knowledge, skills, and desire to serve their Lord as he deserves." Again, "God means every Christian without exception to have a ministry, and the Equipment Room exists to help people discover, and develop, their abilities and gifts of service."

The basic foundation course of the Equipment Room is known as *Core Year.* It offers a much more thorough groundwork than the Annual Training School, which it has superseded, for it consists of thirty complete evenings, one a week throughout three ten-week terms.

Term 1 concentrates on "The Teaching of the Bible," since the Bible is the Christian worker's essential tool, and in particular on those aspects of its teaching which are most needed in witnessing and counseling. These are the Bible itself (its reliability and authority), Jesus Christ (who he was and is), the Gospel (what lies at its heart), Assurance (knowing that you are accepted), the Church (its priceless benefits and stringent demands), Providence (can we believe, or even understand, it?), the Holy Spirit (untangling the confusion), the World (its glories and its snares), Sexual Morality (a firm Christian stance), and the Cross and Resurrection (forgiveness and victory).

Term 2 focuses on "the Interpretation of the Bible," which has increasingly been recognized as a key contemporary issue. Each evening is divided into two periods, first a "principles session" (which gives students a basic method of interpretation, and handles topics like "the sentence in context," "historical background," "words," "types," "prophecy and symbolism," and "application") and then a "practice session," in which the principles are applied to particular passages of Scripture.

Term 3 is the practical one. The Core Year students are now divided into smaller groups, according to their own choice, each of which studies a specific form of Christian service. In 1980, for example, six main areas of ministry were selected: (1) the teaching of children in Sunday School, (2) the leadership of a Beginners' Group (as the former "Nursery Classes" for new converts are now called), (3) Fellowship Group leadership, (4) Christian writing, (5) Evangelistic outreach, and (6) Counseling (not so much in crisis situations as responding with Christian sensitivity to people and their needs).

The training is not given only in old-fashioned lecture form, but includes the use of an overhead projector, discussion, group work, private study, prayer, and role play. Homework is also set each week, which takes two to three hours to complete and is graded at least twice a term. Andrew Cornes is convinced, and the students agree with him, "that half the value of the course is in the disciplined work people do in their own homes." "Gone are the balmy days," he adds, "when no one really checked up on whether you had done your homework or not. . . . You cannot be commissioned unless you fulfill the termly requirement." In fact, the weekly homework has replaced the old written exam.

In addition to the evening sessions and the homework, two weekend house-parties are arranged each year, at which Core Year students can both get to know one another and consider some of the spiritual essentials for effective Christian service.

The response to Core Year has been overwhelming. For each of its first four years of operation the full complement of 120 students has enrolled, and a waiting list has been created. A growing number of people from other churches are also applying to join, in some cases sent by their own minister. So in January 1980 Lance Pierson was appointed as Extension Editor in order to produce a Core Year Extension Program for use in other churches. Twelve churches of different kinds tried out a first pilot version, and a second version is being tested in 1981–82. After Easter 1982 the final version will be produced and should be available by Christmas that year. (Inquiries should be addressed to the Director of Training, All Souls Church, 2 All Souls Place, London W1N 3DB).

There is still an annual Commissioning, in which each person is commissioned to a specific task. Michael Baughen, as senior pastor, commissions them by the laying on of hands, and those in charge of particular areas of service (e.g. the Sunday School superintendent) pray for those being commissioned to serve in their area. The earlier rather rigid distinction between the commissioned and the uncommissioned was understandably felt to be unhealthy and has been abolished, for *every* church member without exception is called to serve. And although people offering for service are urged to enroll in Core Year, no area of ministry is restricted to Core Year graduates (as "Commissioned Workers" are now called). Moreover, commissioning is recognized as being to "a lifetime of service." There is no question, therefore, of "resigning" a commission; only of transferring it to another area of service or to another church.

The areas of ministry in which Core Year graduates can serve are even more diverse than previously. There are still the same opportunities in Sunday School teaching, open youth club work, door-to-door visitation, the leading of Beginners' Groups and Fellowship Groups, old people's visiting, counseling, and help with the International Fellowship. But new avenues of service include the flourishing "Agnostics Anonymous" groups, Christian writing and Christian speaking, hospital visiting, work with students, marriage preparation, manning the church's "Welcome Desk," and evangelistic witnessing in Oxford Street, one of Europe's busiest shopping centers.

One final but important point: Core Year, commissioning, and the resultant service are not the end of the road. It is acknowledged that Core Year graduates need further in-service training. So for those involved in each area of service (e.g. the Sunday School teachers, the Fellowship Group leaders, and the door-to-door visitors) ongoing specialist training sessions are arranged.

Then there is "Second Thoughts," which is an annual course designed for those whose gifts of leadership have come to be recognized. A small group of up to a dozen is involved. Like Core Year, "Second Thoughts" consists of three 10-week terms, but it aims—mainly through discussion—to help participants to submit themselves (their minds and lives) yet more radically to biblical scrutiny and reformation. Members of the group conduct weekends in other churches for evangelism, training or renewal, already occupy positions of responsibility in All Souls Church, and are likely in the future to become team leaders, Sunday School superintendents or lay pastors, or to offer for the ordained ministry.

This leads me to mention Andrew Cornes' latest brainchild, known as ASCAT or the All Souls College of Applied Theology. "We believe so strongly in providing full-time training for those considering a future as clergy, parish workers or missionaries," he writes, "that we are launching a brand new theological college." His vision represents, moreover, an important new departure. For though the theological education given in ASCAT will be just as rigorous as in other institutions, "it will all be done in the real life context of a church, and all the teaching, in lectures and tutorials, will not be discussing ideas for their own sake, but will be relating every area of biblical truth to the needs of men and women in the twentieth century, thus ensuring that all our theology is *applied*." The college has now opened with the first small batch of students, and we all expect that it will grow.

4

The Christian Fellowship

(*koinonia*)

We began by insisting that a proper understanding of the laity depends on a proper understanding of the Church, and that the primary purpose of the biblical church-metaphors is to illustrate not the relations of clergy and laity within the Church but the relations of all God's people to himself and to each other. The latter, our mutual relations as Christian people, are usually referred to in terms of "fellowship," and it is on the meaning and implications of the Christian fellowship that we shall concentrate in this final chapter.

"Fellowship" is an overworked word in the contemporary Church, and the image conveyed by it is often a false image. Indeed, the vocabulary of fellowship has become such devalued currency that it seldom means more than a genial friendliness, what Methodists call a "P.S.A." (Pleasant Sunday Afternoon), or a good gossipy get-together over a nice cup of tea. As a result, we fall sadly short of the rich, deep, full fellowship envisaged in the New Testament.

Yet strong forces are at work toward its recovery—biblical, historical and practical.

ARGUMENTS FOR FELLOWSHIP

To begin with, we have good biblical warrant for asserting that it is not good for man to be alone[1]—an affirmation which at least Calvin saw had a wider reference than to marriage. Aloneness is not the will of God either in ordinary life or in the Christian life. People need fellowship (which we shall still for the moment leave undefined), and it is God's will that they should have it. "The real menace to life in the world today," wrote M. E. Macdonald "is not the hydrogen bomb . . . but the fact of proximity without community."[2]

Bruce Larson, a leader of the American "Faith at Work" movement, sees an indication of this fundamental human need in the popularity of the pub:

> The neighborhood bar is possibly the best counterfeit there is to the fellowship Christ wants to give his Church. It's an imitation, dispensing liquor instead of grace, escape rather than reality, but it is a permissive, accepting and inclusive fellowship. It is unshockable. It is democratic. You can tell people secrets and they usually don't tell others or even want to. The bar flourishes not because most people are alcoholics, but because God has put into the human heart the desire to know and be known, to love and be loved, and so many seek a counterfeit at the price of a few beers. Christ wants his Church to be unshockable, democratic, permissive—a fellowship where people can come in and say "I'm sunk!" "I'm beat!" "I've had it!" Alcoholics Anonymous has this quality. Our churches too often miss it.[3]

But this basic, biblically recognized need is not completely met by Sunday churchgoing or even the larger midweek meetings of the church. There is always something unnatural and subhuman about large crowds. They tend to be aggregations rather than congregations—aggregations of unrelated persons. The larger they become, the less the individuals who compose them know and care about each other. Indeed, crowds can actually perpetuate aloneness, instead of curing it. There is a need, therefore, for large congregations to be divided into smaller groups, such as one imagines the house-churches were in New Testament days.[4] The value of the small group is that it can become a community of related persons; and in it the benefit of personal relatedness cannot be missed, nor its challenge evaded.

This is true of the human family. Our growth into maturity, according to the purpose of God, takes place in the context of a family group. It is the complex pattern of relationships between parents, children, brothers and sisters which, more than anything else, governs our development into adult stature. It is the only child who often suffers, although even in his case there is a unit of three, not to mention relatives, neighbors and friends. Similarly, it is the lone member of the congregation, who holds himself aloof from a more intimate Christian fellowship, who is likely to stunt or damage his spiritual progress.

I do not think it is an exaggeration to say, therefore, that small groups, Christian family or fellowship groups, are indispensable for our growth into spiritual maturity. The preservation of lone-wolf Christianity is perfectly possible for the churchgoer who sits isolated in a pew or hides behind a pillar, even if he attends a so-called midweek "fellowship" where large numbers again gather. His baptism has made him a member of the visible community. By his church attendance he becomes an outwardly conforming member. But still he may not truly belong either to Christ or to the people of Christ.

Turning from a biblical to a historical argument for small groups, we may say that many famous movements of the Spirit of God have either begun or expressed themselves in the intimacy of such fellowship. This is certainly true of the English Reformation, whose roots can be traced to the group of scholars who met in the White Horse Inn in Cambridge to study Erasmus'

Greek Testament. It is also true of Methodism, whether one thinks of the original Holy Club in Oxford or of the class meetings of the developed Society. Reference could also be made to the Praying Societies of Scotland and to the fellowship meetings of the current East African revival. It is from such small and unpretentious beginnings that great movements have sprung up and spread.

The third argument is pastoral. In every congregation of any size there is a need for better and more personal pastoral oversight. The clergy tend to concentrate on nurturing the new convert, visiting the sick, interviewing those to be baptized, confirmed or married, comforting the bereaved, counseling those who ask for help and training workers for witness. But they cannot hope to see or visit every member of their congregation regularly, at least if it is at all sizeable. Nor indeed should they. The pastoral oversight of the congregation does not belong exclusively to the ordained ministry. The Church of Scotland is quite right to have lay elders who share this responsibility with the minister, and one admires the enterprise of the Rev. Roy Henderson who introduced a lay eldership scheme when he was vicar of St. Luke's, Barton Hill, Bristol. He wrote in the *Church of England Newspaper* on 9 June 1967: "We have lay elders who have been duly appointed by the bishop to share in the leadership and pastoral care of the parish." With one exception they are local men already well known to and respected by the congregation.

Moreover, the Bible indicates that each of us is his brother's keeper. It even hints that in one sense every Christian may be regarded as a bishop, because a certain *episcope* ("oversight") is entrusted to every member of the congregation. "See to it," we are told in Hebrews 12:15, where the verb is *episkopountes,* "that no one fail to obtain the grace of God." If this is so, it is in fellowship groups that the ideal can become a reality, for in these the minister delegates some *episcope* or pastoral oversight to the lay leaders, and all learn to care for each.

This is what John Wesley found. On 25 April 1742 he recorded in his Journal:

> I appointed several earnest and sensible men to meet me, to whom I showed the great difficulty I had long found of knowing the people who desired to be under my care. After much discourse, they all agreed there could be no better way to come to a sure, thorough knowledge of each person than to divide them into classes, like those at Bristol, under the inspection of those in whom I could most confide. This was the origin of our classes at London, for which I can never sufficiently praise God, the unspeakable usefulness of the institution having ever since been more and more manifest.[5]

And Dr. R. W. Dale commented on this procedure:

> Methodism made one striking and original contribution to the institutions of the Church, in the Class-meeting. Never, so far as I know, in any church had there been so near an approach to the ideal of pastoral oversight as the Class-meeting, in its perfect form, provides; and it also provides for that communion of saints which is almost as necessary for the strength and joy and the harmonious growth of the Christian life as fellowship with God.[6]

Certainly in our own generation, at least since the end of the Second World War, the house-church or home-group movement has been steadily gathering momentum in many parts of the world. In most cases it has no articulated biblical, historical or pastoral rationale. It seems to be largely spontaneous, a genuine movement of the Holy Spirit. If it needs to be explained in terms of human experience, it is probably to be understood as a protest against the dehumanizing processes of secular society and the superficial formalism of much church life. There is a widespread hunger for a life which is genuinely human and absolutely real.

One such spontaneous movement has been taking place among business and professional people in southwest Texas. Keith Miller wrote about it in *The Taste of New Wine* (1963). His

book's title expresses the heady experience of Christian commitment. These laymen are "no longer satisfied merely to sit in the
pews and on committees or even to stand in pulpits" (p. 18).
Their new life in Christ is like new and fermenting wine, which
threatens to burst the old wineskins of the institutional church
(pp. 105–116). In particular, these men are seeking to live their
lives whole and not to departmentalize their Christianity. "Christ
is tearing out the partitions in men's souls between vocation,
church, and home, and making a one-room dwelling place for
himself in their whole lives" (p. 18). Keith Miller describes the
shock it was when, after he had been a church member and
church worker for many years, a business colleague said to him
"Gee, Keith, I didn't know you were a Christian":

> This stunned me into realizing that, although I had taken Christ by
> the hand and led Him through one passage after another in the lab-
> yrinth of my soul, I had always left Him at the parking lot when I
> drove in to go to my office in the major oil company for which I
> worked (p. 79).

It came to him that the lordship of Christ must be allowed to
penetrate every part of his life:

> I didn't have to have a separate vocabulary, a different kind of
> humor and a different set of ethics for my business life, my church
> life, my family life, and my prayer life (p. 65).

So he invited eleven or twelve people "who seemed most hungry
to know God" to join him in a group. Together they determined
to make the experiment "to take Christ consciously through the
routine of our days and nights" and to report back to one another. Each time they met, they engaged in Bible study and
prayer, but in addition they shared "the problems and discover-
ies" of the past week, and so began to trace "the fresh and con-

temporary footprints of Christ" in their own lives (p. 70, 71). Individually they became involved in visiting the sick, in questions of integration and business life, in the fostering of a Cuban refugee boy and in the after-care of prisoners. But the greatest discovery they made was that Christianity is

> not a "religion" at all, but *real* creative life, life in which we are free to be honest about ourselves, and to accept and love each other and him, because the Living Christ is in the midst of us . . . winning us to himself and to his world (p. 75).

I had the pleasure of meeting Keith Miller in Texas in January 1968 and of hearing him amplify what I had read in his book. What intrigued us both was that we in London had brought into being similar groups with similar aims, although we had begun from the other end. That is to say, Keith Miller and his friends had formed their groups out of a felt need, whereas we (though also aware of the need) had done so from theological conviction, from a study of what the New Testament means by *koinonia*, fellowship.

THE BIBLICAL MEANING OF *KOINONIA*

At the heart of *koinonia* is the basic word *koinos*, "common." And the nouns *koinonia* (fellowship) and *koinonos* (a partner), together with the verb *koinoneo* (to share) all bear witness to what we have in common. Thus C. H. Dodd writes: *"koinonoi* are persons who hold property in common, partners or shareholders in a common concern."[7]

A careful study of the New Testament use of this word-group indicates that Christian *koinonia* or "commonness" takes three forms.

First and foremost, there is what we share in together, our

common Christian inheritance. Indeed this is the fundamental meaning of the word. In usual parlance today "fellowship" describes something subjective, an awareness or an experience of belonging together. "We had good fellowship together," we say, indicating our sense of warmth and security in each other's company. But in the Bible "fellowship" is an objective fact. *Koinonia* bears witness to our common possession of the blessings of the gospel. We have a "common faith" and therefore a "common salvation," being "joint partakers (*sugkoinonous*) of grace."[8] Faith, salvation and grace are the common denominator among Christians; each of us has been saved by grace through faith.[9] It is this that makes us one.

In particular, we share in the saving grace of the three persons of the Trinity. Thus, through the witness of the apostles we come to have fellowship with them, and their fellowship is "with the Father and with his Son Jesus Christ."[10] Indeed, our "fellowship with one another" is dependent on our "fellowship with him."[11] Next, we have been "called" by God "into the fellowship of his Son, Jesus Christ our Lord," and through the breaking of the loaf and the blessing of the cup we enjoy a communion or participation (*koinonia*) in his body and blood.[12] Further, we are granted "the fellowship of the Holy Spirit," who dwells in all the people of God and makes them "partakers (*koinonoi*) of the divine nature."[13]

Begotten by the will and word of the same Father, redeemed by the blood of the same Son, indwelt by the presence of the same Spirit—this is our *koinonia,* the "common salvation" in which we have all come by grace through faith to share.

Not that we can now relax in sloth or sin. For such fellowship with God who is light is itself an incentive to holiness, precluding fellowship with or participation in "the unfruitful works of darkness."[14] Moreover, salvation does not exempt us from suffering. On the contrary, fellowship with Christ includes "the fellowship of his sufferings." But those who "share Christ's sufferings" will also share in "the glory that is to be revealed," so that all Christians are companions in, or partakers (in Jesus) of, both "the tribulation and the kingdom and the patient endurance."[15]

Such is the fundamental meaning of *koinonia,* a common participation in grace now and in glory hereafter, though also of suffering meanwhile. Christian fellowship is our common share in God's "great salvation."[16]

But fellowship is more than what we share *in* together. There is also, and secondly, what we share *out* together. For *koinonia* in the New Testament concerns not only what we possess but what we do together, not only our common inheritance but also our common service. Luke uses the word *koinonoi* to describe the business relationship between the two pairs of brothers James and John, Andrew and Simon. They were "partners," he says.[17] C. H. Dodd explains this as meaning that they were "joint owners of the little fishing fleet," but it surely means also that they were colleagues, engaged together in the same fishing trade.

After the apostles had successfully landed their great netful of fish, Jesus said to Simon "Do not be afraid; henceforth you will be catching men." It is perhaps, therefore, not too fanciful to regard the church as a great fellowship of fishermen, *koinonoi,* partners with Jesus Christ and with one another in the business of catching men. Certainly Paul refers to his co-laborers Titus and Philemon as his *koinonoi,* and specially mentions how Philemon shared out his faith with others.[18] But it was not only such Christian leaders who were Paul's companions in labor. He could thank God for the Philippian Christians' "partnership in the Gospel," which had persisted "from the first day" (of their conversion) until the time of his writing to them.[19] The preposition *eis* (rendered here "in") makes it plain that their partnership was in the spread of the Gospel, not just in the enjoyment of its benefits. A similar use of the word *koinonia* in relation to the preaching of the Gospel occurs in Galatians 2:9. Here Paul describes how the Jerusalem apostles, James, Peter, and John, gave to him and to Barnabas "the right hand of fellowship." What did this gesture indicate? It was a token of partnership in world evangelization, signifying "that we should go to the Gentiles and they to the circumcised."

The gospel is not the only treasure, however, which Christians have to share out together. Another is our material possessions. Rich people are to be specially *koinonikos* "generous,"[20] and all Christians are told not to neglect *koinonia*,[21] but rather to "contribute (*koinoneo*) to the needs of the saints."[22] And *koinonia* is the word Paul employs for the "contribution" of the Macedonian and Achaian churches to the poor saints at Jerusalem.[23] Thus *koinonia* seems to express as much our joint-communication of, as our joint-participation in, the blessings of the Gospel.

In these first two aspects of *koinonia,* which we have been considering, one might say that Christian people are all facing in one of two directions. When we concentrate on what we share in or possess together, we are all facing the Lord who has given himself to us. When we concentrate on what we share out or do together, we are all facing other people—either the world or the church—whom we are seeking to serve. But the third aspect of *koinonia* concerns what we share with one another, and when we concentrate on this we are no longer facing in the same direction: we are gathered in a circle, facing each other. Dr. Fitchett once reminded a Canadian audience that

> there are two ideas of the religious life. There is the tramcar idea and the fireside idea. In the tramcar you sit beside your fellow-passenger. You are all going in the same direction, but you have no fellowship, no intercourse with or interest in one another. . . . Then there is the fireside, where the family meet together, where they are at home, where they converse one with another of common pursuits and common interests, and where a common relationship binds all together in a warm bond of love and fellowship. . . . Methodism stands for the fireside idea.[24]

But the "fireside idea" should not be allowed to be a Methodist monopoly. It is an indispensable characteristic of New Testament *koinonia.* This is not a fellowship in which we are all recipients or all givers, but what Paul calls a "partnership . . . in giving and receiving"[25]—a verse of Scripture which would have made an admirable text for the Anglican program of MRI (Mutual Responsibility and Interdependence).[26]

This kind of fellowship may be said to have begun on the Day of Pentecost. When Luke wrote of the newly created, believing, Spirit-filled community that they "had all things in common,"[27] he meant that they shared with each other what they had. It was a fellowship of giving and receiving. It would be a mistake, however, to suppose that this third expression of *koinonia* is exclusively concerned with money. For example, the giving and receiving which had taken place between Paul and the Philippians was that he had given them the Gospel, while they had sent him a present.[28] Similarly, although the collection among the Greek churches for the poor saints of Judaea was in one sense a freewill offering, it was also the repayment of a debt. Paul saw it as a meaningful symbol of Jewish-Gentile "MRI," "for if the Gentiles have come to share in their spiritual blessings, they ought also to be of service to them in material blessings."[29]

Paul had a strong sense of this mutual responsibility and interdependence between Christians and churches. Although he was himself an apostle of Jesus Christ, bearing Christ's name and Gospel before the Gentiles, he was humble enough to acknowledge his need of what others could give him. His Master had once asked an immoral Samaritan woman to give him a drink of water; and Paul often confessed his need of human friendship.[30] So too in writing to the Romans, although he does not here use the vocabulary of *koinonia,* he says that he longed to visit them not only to impart some spiritual gift to them to strengthen them, but also "that we may be mutually encouraged by each other's faith, both yours and mine."[31]

It is in this connection that we need to consider the many "one another" verses of the New Testament, which describe the reciprocity of true Christian fellowship.

The commonest use of *allelous* "one another" is of reciprocal love. Jesus said: "A new commandment I give to you, that you love one another; even as I have loved you, that you also love one another. By this all men will know that you are my disciples, if you have love for one another." He repeated the command a little later,[32] and we hear echoes of it in the apostolic letters of Paul, Peter, and John.[33]

All the remaining "one another" verses of the New Testament are the outworking—negative and positive—of this mutual love. If we love one another we shall not "judge" one another, nor "bite," "devour," "provoke" or "envy" one another, nor "lie" to one another, nor "speak evil against" or "grumble against" one another.[34] True love for one another will express itself positively in a desire to build one another up. This will include "receiving" one another, being "kind" and "tenderhearted" towards one another, forbearing and forgiving one another, "serving" one another, practicing "hospitality" ungrudgingly to one another, admonishing or instructing one another, submitting to one another, and comforting one another in bereavement.[35]

All this active, purposive service of one another arises from the fundamental fact that we belong to one another. We *are* our brother's keeper precisely because we are brothers. Or, to employ Paul's favorite metaphor, "we, though many, are one body in Christ, and individually members one of another."[36] Therefore we must serve one another with the gifts we have received, neither envying nor despising one another, "that there may be no discord in the body, but that the members may have the same care for one another." Then, "if one member suffers, all suffer together; if one member is honored, all rejoice together."[37]

Such "membership one of another" and mutual caring can be expressed only when the members meet in fellowship. So "greet one another" is another reciprocal duty often repeated in the New Testament epistles,[38] even if the "holy kiss" with which we do it is today replaced by what J. B. Phillips calls "a handshake all round, please." If we do not neglect to meet, but actually come together in fellowship, then we are able to "consider how to stir up one another to love and good works."[39] Then too we can confess our sins to one another, if we have offended one another, and "pray for one another."[40] Again, we can "bear one another's burdens, and so fulfill the law of Christ," for we can "rejoice with those who rejoice" and "weep with those who weep."[41] All this rich and varied "one anotherness" is an essential part of what the New Testament means by "fellowship."

Let me now summarize the threefold aspect which *koinonia* wears in the New Testament. It speaks of our common inheritance (what we share in together), of our cooperative service (what we share out together) and of our reciprocal responsibility (what we share with one another). In the first we are receiving together, in the second we are giving together, while in the third there is a mutual give and take.

BIBLICAL THEORY AND PAROCHIAL PRACTICE

This is the biblical theory. But an increasing number of Christian people are finding the theory workable. Consider, for example, what has been happening in the Diocese of Coventry since the consecration of its new cathedral. Stephen Verney calls his paperback *Fire in Coventry* "a book about the Holy Spirit" (p. 9). It begins with a moving account of how the clergy of Monks Kirby, a suburb of Coventry, became "a team of men who knew one another, cared about one another, belonged to one another, and most important of all, had begun to admit to one another their own weaknesses" (p. 14). Then their experience of fellowship spread, in successive ripples, reaching both clergy and laity throughout the diocese. Its three elements are analyzed as love (which "goes out to the last and the lost and the least," p. 33), prayer (men putting themselves at God's disposal) and the Holy Spirit. "These are the three who dance together and are one at the heart of the Church—Love, Prayer, the Holy Spirit. All else is secondary" (p. 51). Stephen Verney depicts them as entering the pages of St. John's Gospel "like three ballet dancers": "Love one another . . . ask in my name . . . I will give you the Spirit of Truth." "First one, then another, holds the center of the stage; they hold hands and dance together; they weave in and out and through one another in intricate patterns." He concludes: "These three dance together and are one, and that one is Jesus Christ. And he gives us all three at once as he gives us himself . . ." (pp. 89, 90).

Perhaps I may illustrate the same biblical theory, but in greater detail, from our experience in London. Once our Parochial Church Council had seen and studied the high ideal of Christian fellowship set forth in the New Testament, we were determined to attempt to turn the theory into practice, and to make the ideal a reality. For fifteen years the central meeting of the church each week had been "the Hour of Prayer." We had seen it grow from an attendance of about twenty to a maximum of about two hundred, and then decrease again to a regular one hundred or so. But we were dissatisfied with it. It had grown stale. Many who led in prayer were inaudible. Further, it tended to be clerically dominated, and it provided no opportunity for mutual fellowship. In a word, the fellowship it expressed was lopsided.

So after careful thought and thorough debate the Church Council reached the unanimous decision to discontinue it and to transfer the weekly intercession of the Hour of Prayer to fortnightly Fellowship Groups in different homes and (in the alternate weeks) to Parish Evenings, to which the groups would be urged to come together.

In April 1965 a policy statement was issued, which began: "The staff, churchwardens and Parochial Church Council have during the last year given a great deal of thought and study to the biblical meaning of Christian fellowship, and to its application to our church life at All Souls. We are convinced from Scripture and history of the importance and value of small Fellowship Groups. And we believe that God is leading us, for the spiritual good of the congregation, to develop them at All Souls. Indeed, so persuaded are we about this, that we mean to give them priority in the church's weekday program. We hope that ultimately every member of the congregation will become a member of a Fellowship Group as well. . . . Our desire is that each Fellowship Group will express and develop the three aspects of Christian fellowship which we find in Scripture, namely our relationship to God himself, our care for one another and our service to the world. We hope and pray that the members of each group will increase in the knowledge of God by corporate devotional Bible reading, and will learn to care for one another in love and bear one another's burdens, and will engage together in some common Christian service."

It may be helpful to see how the Fellowship Groups are attempting to fulfill this threefold ideal.

First, every Fellowship Group seeks to give expression to the common life which its members already enjoy, and to deepen and enrich it. The chief means to this end is devotional Bible reading and prayer. Every six months or so a suggested list of short Bible passages is produced, either consecutive or topical, sometimes with a few explanatory notes. This list is duplicated in sufficient quantity for every member to have a copy, so that some preparatory reading of the passage is possible. It is emphasized, however, that the Fellowship Group is not a Bible study class, that the Bible reading must not therefore dominate the evening, and that the leader's responsibility is not to lecture the group. Instead, the task of the leaders (who are nearly all lay men and women) is to help the group to feed upon Christ together in and through his Word. Their object in reading is not just to understand what the passage means, but to go beyond its meaning to its message, to allow it to speak to our situation, to direct and correct us, to exhort, rebuke, challenge or comfort us. We emphasize that the reading of God's Word is never an end itself, but a means to a deeper knowledge of God himself and to a more obedient conformity to his Will.

Many hazards threaten the profit of this Bible reading time. The garrulous have to be restrained and the silent ones encouraged to speak. And the method of meditation has to be varied if monotony is to be avoided, now by looking through the passage verse by verse, now by selective reading, now by question and answer. Several leaders invite members of their group to take turns in leading. All try to encourage a relaxed, non-classroom atmosphere.

Once a year most of the Fellowship Groups receive Holy Communion in the room in which they meet. We have used a simple service in modern language, and the clergy have not worn robes. This has been a precious time of corporate feeding on Christ in sacrament as well as Scripture, since he makes himself known to us not only in his Word, but also in the breaking of bread.

Most groups "break bread" informally also, enjoying a simple form of "agape" or "love feast" each time they meet. In some cases it is only a cup of tea and a biscuit; in others it is a full meal. In either case the addition of the social to the spiritual tends to deepen the fellowship.

Secondly, the Fellowship Groups are seeking to extend their fellowship of "sharing out" as well as of "sharing in," for a Fellowship Group which is entirely inward-looking becomes ingrowing, unhealthy and sterile. Indeed, "sharing in" and "sharing out" belong together, and each becomes unbalanced without the other. Another way of putting the same thing is that the Christian is called both to "holiness" and to "worldliness," both to withdrawal and to involvement. Further, fruitful Christian involvement in the world is impossible without the spiritual resources which withdrawal supplies, while these resources (gained in withdrawal) are given to be expended in service in the world. Dr. Elton Trueblood applies this truth to the church's common life. He defines the Church as "a fellowship of consciously inadequate persons who gather because they are weak, and scatter to serve because their unity with one another and with Christ has made them bold."[42] Again, "we are making a great step forward when we realize that there is no inevitable contradiction between the idea of the scattered church and the idea of the gathered church. We gather in order to scatter!"[43]

What service, then, do Fellowship Groups perform? To begin with, each group is engaged in intercession, which can rightly be understood as common service, reaching out in prayer to embrace the whole world. This was emphasized in the policy statement already mentioned: "During each Fellowship Group . . . there will be a half-hour of prayer, stimulated and guided . . . by parochial and missionary prayer topics. Some people have spoken with regret of the death of the Hour of Prayer, which for years has been the church's most important midweek meeting. This is more than understandable. The Council emphasizes, however, that what is proposed is only the transformation of a particular form of prayer service into something else and something better. It will mean not the death of prayer, but rather its resurrection. Under the new scheme, many more people will, in fact, be praying than before. Moreover, the praying will be more audible, more natural, more intimate, and therefore, we believe, more effective. Let there be no mistake about it: we still intend to put prayer first, and we believe that our serious intercession as a congregation is going in the future to be considerably increased, improved and enriched."

I think we can claim that this has proved to be true. One elderly and experienced man of prayer has described the change as "a real blessing to the whole congregation." A list of suggested prayer topics is duplicated each fortnight, relating to the work of the church and parish. In most groups these are read aloud by a member, while the rest listen or take notes, but a few groups like all their members to have the duplicated sheet so that they may take it home with them afterward and continue to use it in their private prayers. Several have said that these topics give them "inside information" about the life of the church and help them to feel more personally involved in it.

Then there is missionary prayer. Each Fellowship Group has "adopted" one or two of our church's missionaries. Group members correspond with them and receive the magazine of their missionary society, so as to keep themselves up-to-date with news from the field. This arrangement has resulted in the formation of really personal bonds between missionaries and the supporting home church. One group has also made and dispatched needed items to a missionary in Uganda, and another has sent books to a missionary who works in a Bible Institute in Chile.

Good Idea!

But we are not content for a Fellowship Group's common service to be limited to intercessory prayer. We believe it should be more than this. It is perhaps easiest for those groups which are composed of people who already work together—whether as visitors, Sunday School teachers or club leaders. Again, when the group is composed of local residents, it is natural for them to become concerned for and involved in the welfare of others living in the same street or block. This has happened with a few of our groups. For example one group, instead of their usual time of fellowship, spent an evening redecorating the apartment of a senior citizen. But most of our groups have an eclectic membership and seek other avenues of service. It must be admitted that several have been unsuccessful—through lack of time or of enterprise. Others, however, have offered their practical services as a group—in the annual springclean of the church, in the door-to-door distribution of leaflets, in street "fishing" before an evening service, in supporting an open-air service and in a visiting "blitz" in another parish. Several groups have also made themselves responsible for the preparing of food, the serving and the dish washing at a parish function—including a Christmas party for overseas visitors, tea-parties for confirmation candidates and university freshmen, a residential Family Service weekend and a number of Parish Evenings. Another group has started a "self-denial" campaign, to stimulate practical concern for the needy people of the world. Certainly without some such common concern and service, the fellowship of any Christian group is maimed.

The third aspect of *koinonia,* sharing with one another, is probably the most difficult to achieve and develop. But if Christians are brothers and sisters in Christ, they should know each other, love each other, take an interest in each other and care for each other. As Bruce Larson has put it: "The Church is meant to be a company of people as committed to one another as to Christ."[44] This was an essential part of the Methodist class meetings. John Wesley wrote in his *Plain Account of the People called Methodists:*

> It can scarce be conceived what advantages have been reaped from this little prudential regulation. Many now happily experienced that Christian fellowship of which they had not so much as an idea before. They began to "bear one another's burdens" and naturally to "care for each other." As they had daily a more intimate acquaintance with, so they had a more endeared affection for, each other. And "speaking the truth in love, they grew up into him in all things who is the Head, even Christ; from whom the whole body, fitly joined together, and compacted by that which every joint supplied, according to the effectual working in the measure of every part, increased unto the edifying of itself in love."[45]

George Whitefield wrote similarly in his *Letter to the Religious Societies:*

> My brethren . . . let us plainly and freely tell one another what God has done for our souls. To this end, you would do well, as others have done, to form yourselves into little companies of four or five each, and meet once a week to tell each other what is in your hearts; that you may then also pray for and comfort each other as need shall require. None but those who have experienced it can tell the unspeakable advantages of such a union and communion of souls. . . . None I think that truly loves his own soul and his breth-

ren as himself, will be shy of opening his heart, in order to have their advice, reproof, admonition and prayers, as occasions require. A sincere person will esteem it one of the greatest blessings.

What Wesley and Whitefield wrote is undoubtedly true, but even sincere persons are sometimes shy, and may find it difficult to be open. In a questionnaire which I recently issued to Fellowship Group members, a number spoke of their personal reserve, and some indicated that they felt "the climate of confidence" was missing which would make such an intimate exchange possible. Indeed, it must be confessed, some groups have acquiesced in the difficulties and abandoned the attempt to foster such sharing. Others, however, have persevered and have been rewarded. One member has written of "the bonds of love and *genuine* interest and concern which have grown up between members over the months." Another refers to the "mutual assistance" he has found; he likens his group to "a rock climber's rope." Another describes the members of the group to which she belongs as "now closely knit together as a family." In answer to the question, "What have you found most helpful in your Fellowship Group?" several have referred to the opportunity to share their thoughts and problems, their doubts and fears, together with blessings received and lessons learned, and one specified "the certainty that the members really care for each other."

So whenever the Fellowship Group meets, the leader is encouraged to make time for an expression of this part of Christian fellowship. Members are given the opportunity to share what is on their hearts. In the questionnaire I asked: "Can you give any example of the group bearing or sharing one of your burdens?" Many could. Several had been prayed for and visited during a period of sickness. Others appreciated the sympathy and prayers of the group in a time of bereavement and loneliness. One could say regarding a time of adversity: "They covered me with prayer in various ways." Others had asked for specific prayer regarding an exam, a new job, the possibility of God's call to be a missionary, the need for accommodation or staff, or some Christian service they were undertaking. A doctor was supported by his group when giving a series of addresses at a Christian medical conference, and a girl while she worked at a holiday camp. Others have shared with their group their concern for sick relatives, and for friends or colleagues they were longing to win for Christ. One group was able to report four conversions among the friends and relatives of its members, in answer to their united intercession. It may be said, therefore, that this ideal of "caring and sharing," and of "bearing one another's burdens," is beginning to be fulfilled. It cannot be artificially induced. But as mutual love grows in a group, mutual care grows with it.

Of course what Wesley called a "prudential regulation" is also a perilous procedure. It exposes frail sinners to the dangers of exhibitionism, hypocrisy and self-pity. But there is safety in numbers—in a Fellowship Group as in a family. There's nothing like a family to knock off our rough corners. They will sympathize with us and stand by us loyally when we are in genuine trouble. But they will stand no nonsense if they think we are trying to exploit them!

THE IDEAL AND THE REALITY

Fellowship Groups are composed of human beings, and all human beings differ from one another. We have no desire, therefore, to stereotype a group's program or development. Nevertheless we believe that true Christian *koinonia* involves the rich and comprehensive sharing which I have tried to unfold. And therefore we constantly keep before our eyes the threefold biblical ideal. We are anxious that the groups will not become unbalanced and degenerate into being merely Bible reading groups or prayer groups or study groups. We want them to be true to their name, "fellowship groups" expressing the fullness of Christian fellowship. So we keep asking ourselves: are we growing in Christian maturity together? Are we serving the Lord, the Church or the world together? Are we increasing in love and care for one another?

"I think the groups are the nucleus and heart of the church," one member wrote. This we increasingly believe, and so try to keep them in the forefront of our thinking. Every person who joins the church is given details of Fellowship Groups and encouraged to join one. And every new Christian who graduates from a Nursery Class is urged to go on to a Fellowship Group.

So each group is seeking to become what Hendrik Kraemer in his book several times calls "a Christocentric, Christocratic brotherhood." But even if Christ is the unseen center and leader of the group, it still needs a human leader. Generally speaking, these are lay people, while members of the church staff circulate, trying to attend a different group every fortnight. This lay leadership of the groups makes possible that delegated *episcope* (pastoral oversight) which we have already seen to be so desirable. Do the lay people resent the lay leadership? Far from it! We pastors may cherish the illusion that we are needed and missed, but the groups consider that they get on better without us! In the questionnaire I asked: "Are you in favor of the lay leadership of the groups?" Ninety-five out of the 108 who answered were in favor. They gave three main reasons. The first was biblical principle, that lay leaders "are sharing in the ministry of the church," that "the gift of spiritual leadership is not conferred by ordination," that such experience "helps to develop the spiritual abilities of the laity," and that "this makes us more aware that we are the church." The second was pastoral necessity, that the clergy do not have time to exercise all the leadership and must therefore share it. And the third reason was rather embarrassingly personal. Lay leaders, the questionnaire answers inform us, are "more human and understanding," particularly because they are themselves living and working in lay situations. Further, as a Korean girl put it candidly, "If clergyman leads group I become selfconscious and reserved." Thirty-three people confessed that they are much more free, relaxed and at ease in the absence of the clergy!

POSTSCRIPT

Having appointed Andrew Cornes as "Director of Training," Michael Baughen went on to appoint Richard Inwood in 1978 as "Director of Pastoring," with special responsibility for the oversight and development of the Fellowship Groups.

The same general pattern has been maintained. That is to say, the committed nucleus of the congregation meets one week in separate Fellowship Groups and the next week together, although a small number of Fellowship Groups meet weekly. The old Parish Evening is now called the "Prayer Gathering" because, though it still combines prayer with the sharing of news, it concentrates on prayer. Michael Baughen has introduced us to the beautiful concept of the congregation as a "church family." He normally presides at the Prayer Gathering and has the unusual ability to make us feel we belong to one another. We worship together in word and song, are fed with a brief exposition of Scripture, welcome back a returned missionary, exchange local, missionary, and global items for prayer, and pray together both in unison (though the average attendance is about 200) and in small groups of half a dozen—an excellent arrangement which enables more people to participate. This coming together of the church family every other week is one of the highlights of our common life.

Under Richard Inwood's leadership the Fellowship Groups have developed a threefold pattern similar to the one I have outlined in the foregoing chapter, though not identical with it. "My rule of thumb," he has written about the groups' evening meeting, which normally lasts for three hours, "is that one hour should be spent in Bible study, one hour in getting to know folk, coming alongside one another and sharing with one another, usually in the context of a meal together, and one hour in sharing needs for prayer and in praying together. Prayer in the groups is also more personally based these days. We encourage people to share as deeply as they are able with their groups, so that they may receive the prayer support of those who should be closest to them spiritually."

The Bible study material is prepared every four months, and nearly all the groups study the same passage each evening. This helps to cement the unity of the church family. Since in every four-month period the groups meet seven or eight times, a New Testament letter or a section of a Gospel can be conveniently divided up for study. Richard Inwood (and now his successor, Mike Lawson) produces notes for the leaders to use in their own preparation, but these are not circulated to all the group members.

The "service" aspect of *koinonia* is sometimes included within the group's meeting. For example, a number of groups have been organizing evangelistic supper parties for their friends and neighbors. But most of the service takes place outside the group evening. Fellowship Groups now take turns cooking lunches and suppers after Sunday morning and evening services respectively, and accept responsibility on a rotation basis for tidying the books in the sanctuary seats after every worship service (a Herculean task!).

When Richard Inwood came, the number of Fellowship Groups was just under fifty; it is now just under eighty. And a recent survey revealed that nearly half the regular congregation belongs to a Fellowship Group.

How are new members recruited? The main way is doubtless the most natural—through established group members inviting their friends to join their group. In addition, however, a "Newcomers' Fellowship Group" has been formed. New members of the church family come to it for one evening only. Its leaders then decide with each newcomer which Fellowship Group will be the most suitable for him or her to join, according to geographical, pastoral, and personal factors, and according to availability of space in the groups. Recently an average of 250 people have passed through this Newcomers' Fellowship Group each year.

Richard Inwood's main contribution to the development of Fellowship Groups has probably been in the pastoral care of the leaders themselves, all but one of whom are lay people. Previously, they all came together twice a year, to meet one another and Michael Baughen. But these meetings became too big, unwieldly and formal. Besides, the Fellowship Group leaders have one of the most important responsibilities in the life of the church. They do not only lead a Bible study; they exercise a pastoral care of their group's members and they also encourage their members in mutual care. So Michael Baughen refers to these leaders as "the corporate pastorate."

Recognizing that these lay pastors needed help in fulfilling their responsible role, Richard Inwood developed a "support group" system. His argument was that "if each individual needs to be in a small group for study, support and prayer, so those with responsibility for leadership of those groups need themselves to be in a group for study, support and prayer." He therefore established seven support groups, each consisting of the leaders of ten Fellowship Groups. Each support group met once a quarter with Richard and his team. These evenings would begin with a meal together. The leaders would then share the problems and joys they had been experiencing in their groups, discuss these with one another and pray about them together. The second half of the evening would be given over to in-service training in some aspect of group leadership, such as counseling, Bible study or prayer in the group.

In addition to the help they receive from their support groups, the Fellowship Group leaders enjoy an annual weekend conference in the country. This gives them an opportunity for spiritual feeding on the Word of God together, for further training through workshops, for the discussion of problems, and so for reciprocal encouragement. In 1981 about one hundred went away together for this time of refreshment.

Additional Bibliography (supplied by Richard Inwood)

Eddie Gibbs: *Grow through Groups* (Grove Booklet on Ministry and Worship, No. 64)

Jimmy Hamilton-Brown: "Study Project on Small Groups in Five Parishes" (Archbishops' Committee on Evangelism, 1979)

Gordon Jones: *Design for Learning* (Falcon, 1974)

Amiel Osmaston: *Sharing the Life* (Grove Booklet on Ministry and Worship, No. 63)

David Prior: *Sharing Pastoral Care in the Parish* (Grove Booklet, Pastoral Series, No. 3)

Clyde Reid: *Groups Alive—Church Alive* (Harper and Row, 1969)

John Tanburn: *Open House* (Falcon, 1970)

5

A North American Perspective

Editor's Note: This chapter is written by the senior pastor of Long Hill Chapel in Chatham, New Jersey, the Reverend Paul F. Bubna.

No doubt some members of the Long Hill Chapel congregation would be surprised to find our church discussed in this book. We certainly can make no claim to having arrived. However, we are a body of believers awakened to the challenge of seeing every member as a minister and we have committed ourselves to move with resolution toward that goal. The fact that we have not arrived may make the telling of our story all the more helpful. It occurs to me that if someone is at point A and wishes to reach point B, he may be helped more by observing someone on the journey than by merely viewing someone who has already arrived.

Long Hill Chapel is a body of believers that meets in Chatham, New Jersey. Chatham, in Morris County, once a summer resort area for metropolitan New Yorkers, is situated about forty-five minutes west of New York City. Though largely populated with commuters, this upper middle-class "bedroom community" retains a good deal of the small town atmosphere.

The Chapel congregation began meeting in a little brick schoolhouse at the top of Long Hill in Chatham in 1945. From its humble beginnings, this church has offered warm fellowship and strong biblical preaching to a growing number of worshipers. In time the congregation outgrew two buildings and constructed a modest-sized sanctuary on Shunpike Road in Chatham Township. The congregation now numbers about twelve hundred people and on a typical Sunday morning approximately nine hundred attend worship service.

The Chapel congregation is a delightful mix of people from varied backgrounds and vocations. However, drawing from a region peopled with a higher than average number of middle and top management men and women, Long Hill Chapel has always enjoyed a strong lay leadership that knows how to plan and execute. For twenty-five years, the congregation thrived under the ministry of a dynamic senior pastor whose biblical preaching and charisma were major factors in the growth and prosperity of the church.

Only when the church began searching for another dynamic leader did the question arise concerning the philosophy of ministry. After months of futile searching for a senior pastor, the boards of the church met to pray and attempt to put in writing the qualities they were looking for in a leader. At this point a concern for the development of the laity began to emerge. Questionnaires were given to all members of the congregation and a study committee appointed to formulate a plan of action.

This study produced a paper that was published on January 12, 1977, and which began with this question, "What has the Lord been teaching us while we have been without a senior pastor the last sixteen months?" The first answer was "to depend upon God rather than primarily one leader, however gifted that leader might be."

As the leaders began to formulate goals for the church, certain biblical concepts became clear. "One primary need is individual commitment to a scriptural life-style by each member of the congregation," noted the study. Another is "a greater degree of spiritual unity within the congregation and the spiritual growth of every believer."

Among the ways listed to accomplish these goals were these: "There needs to be more small group prayer and Bible study and sharing activities, more discipling by pastoral staff and lay leaders, more encouraging each other on a one-to-one basis, and more cultivation of individual spiritual gifts. Discipleship, for example, through retreats or other long-range planning sessions by the leadership or through more follow-up and visitation by individual church members. In all of the church activities the example and direction set by the lay and pastoral leadership as well as the shepherding care of the pastoral staff are crucial."

Most interesting was the description of the senior pastor whom they were seeking. "A pastor/teacher with a strong, positive pulpit ministry centered in the Word of God, but also a man who could build and disciple a team of other leaders to motivate and encourage the laity of the church." This crisis of pastoral change proved to be a significant hour in the development of the Long Hill congregation. It caused the church to define clearly its biblical goals and, in doing so, catch a glimpse of what it means for the local church to be One People.

I am just finishing my fourth year as senior pastor of the Chapel. It has been a stimulating and growing experience. When I first came here to meet with the officers of the congregation, it was soon evident that these people had caught a vision and were enthused about pursuing it. While they did not use those exact words, they were looking for a leader who would help them become One People. This is how this journey has looked from my perspective.

SEEING THE CONCEPT

The congregation I had previously served had been working toward the goal of every member being a minister. If you had asked me at that point how I viewed the role of the pastor, I would have used the metaphor of Elton Trueblood; the pastor is a player/coach. He is to play the game and teach others how to play also. This had been a commitment made and a concept growing in my heart for a number of years. However, Long Hill Chapel is a large and highly structured church with strong leadership. But, while they saw themselves as running the business and organization of the church, I think most of the leaders would have agreed that the ministry was done by the pastor and his staff.

Though the idea of a ministering laity was a growing concept at Long Hill Chapel, the real impetus had to come from among these leaders. And since the pastor is looked upon as the key leader in the local church, change had to begin with me. I saw that I needed to be totally committed to this concept. It had to so completely grip my heart and mind that all my plans, goals and objectives would be shaped and flavored by it.

As Dr. Stott has stated well, the ministry of the laity begins as a whole new way of looking at the church. It is seeing the church as a community of people, all of whom are joined together by the call of God upon their lives. They must see themselves as one church, one people, joined organically to Jesus Christ. If that idea is to possess a local body of believers, it must possess the heart of its leadership and especially its pastor. It occurs to me that one of the most important things about a local church is the picture that the pastor has in his mind regarding the nature of the Body of Christ. If that is a picture of a false division between clergy and laity, that approach will come across in a thousand different ways—in sermons, in plans, in conversations, in subtle attitudes. In short, the pastor has to put on new glasses so that he can begin to see it all from a New Testament perspective.

LEADING BY EXAMPLE

While a concept needs to be constantly and clearly verbalized, it is still evident that ideas are more caught than taught. While in no way diminishing my call to be an expositor of the Word and to proclaim it with authority, I saw that if Long Hill Chapel was to become a ministering body of saints then I must not be merely one who instructs them from a distance, but one who walks beside them and serves as an enabler and equipper. This involves relationships. It involves not merely sharing one's ministry, but really giving it away. If the local church is to be an open, caring fellowship of believers, that concept must be demonstrated in the way that the senior pastor relates to the other members of the pastoral staff. And further than that, it must be created in microcosm among the boards and committees of the church as they meet together.

Committee meetings need to be seen not merely as decision-making convocations but as prayer meetings, as times for the members of the body to encourage, affirm, and motivate each other to love and good works. A concept begins to impact our lives as it is lived out in relationships.

Evangelism lies at the center of the church's commitment as Christ's Body in the world. However, the congregation as a ministering body not only becomes the environment for equipping witnesses, but its life-style of loving service validates its witness before the world (*see* John 13:35).

STARTING SMALL

Probably one of the most important lessons, and one learned with difficulty, is that if there is to be a change in concept it has to begin small. This requires patience and faith. It takes time to build deep and personal relationships in which one's life and ministry can be shared with another person. When one lives and works among busy executives who give their time to the local church at no small sacrifice, the opportunity for personal exposure needs to be used carefully and wisely. However, the main ingredient is to keep one's eye on the goal and to patiently plod along letting relationships develop naturally so that one's own inner life can be built into the lives of others. When church committees meet only once a month, change comes very slowly.

Larry Richards points out in his book *New Face for the Church* that we must bring change in concept first and structure later. Concept has to be lived out by example. That means starting small and letting it begin to catch on. As a new idea is lived out among the leaders and committees of the church body, it begins to permeate the whole and then to take form naturally in the existing structures of the body. When those structures need to be changed because of the new life that begins to surge, the church will allow those changes to be made in a very natural way.

In a success-oriented society where big is beautiful, the pastor is under constant pressure to merely organize people and use them to get things done rather than to take time to use the work to build people into effective ministers. It seems like such a subtle difference, but in the long run the pastor will be tempted to use his energy to merely organize and build a successful machine rather than taking the time to walk personally beside people and pursue the goal of enabling them to be God's ministers.

However, when the pastor sets his heart to be a servant leader, when his heartfelt goal is to see God's people become successful in their ministry, it does begin to multiply over a period of time. More than that, a strategy begins to develop out of the leadership of the local church which allows the dynamics that God intends to be present in church to manifest themselves in a natural way.

Here are some of the ways that *diakonia, marturia,* and *koinonia* are beginning to express themselves among the laity of Long Hill Chapel.

The rapid growth of the Long Hill congregation made it necessary to hire additional pastors for the staff. However, it became increasingly evident that even an enlarged staff could not adequately shepherd such a large body of believers. Out of this awareness there began to emerge a new way of looking at the elders. Though our elders were godly men from many walks of life, because of the upper management culture of our area, it was

[handwritten margin note: GOOD POINT!]

easy to think of the eldership as an administrative position with its attending recognition.

It became evident, however, that not only must the elders see themselves as serving leaders, but they must use their gifts to lead others to become ministers so that the whole congregation might be adequately shepherded to spiritual growth. To become a ministering body we needed leaders who serve, and this necessitated training.

Out of all of this emerged the idea of creating a large body of committed leaders who would be willing to accept training and commit themselves to serve. The deacons and deaconesses are appointed by the Board of Elders and are an extension of its ministry. This past year, over twenty men were appointed as deacons. The intention is for this number to be continually expanding. These men meet once a month with a member of the pastoral staff to study together and prepare themselves to be ministers. This involves the reading of books about the concepts of the local church, leadership, personal and spiritual growth, and Bible study.

The deacons are appointed to serve on each of the elder committees. The ministry that used to be carried on solely by elders is now performed by committees that are mostly made up of deacons with the leadership of one or more elders. This has expanded and enriched the capabilities of our Elder Board.

The deaconesses have, likewise, begun to spend more time in worship and discipleship during their meetings. With the deacons, they are learning that service is not something to be done by the exclusive few but rather something to be given away and multiplied through humble service.

The multiplying of our ministers opens the door for broad impact, both within the local body and the larger community. Ministry to rescue missions, nursing homes, and state mental hospitals are the overflow of the concept of every member being a minister.

As a means of shepherding such a large congregation and at

the same time providing a basis of identification and fellowship, we formed CARE groups. The word "CARE" is an acronym for *C*ongregations *A*ffirming, *R*elating, *E*ncouraging.

After two years, probably over half of our adults are now committed members of a CARE group, each numbering between fifteen to twenty people. They meet each month in a home where they are able to talk together about their personal lives, needs, and, most of all, about their attachment to Jesus Christ. The CARE groups are led by two couples who endeavor, by their example and involvement with the various members of their group, to engender a sense of caring and congregation.

Each meeting of the CARE group usually involves some Bible study and structured involvement. However, the main intent is to build a sense of community where the gospel finds practical expression by touching the lives of other people.

In times of crisis the effectiveness of the CARE group is most evident. When someone loses a loved one, their CARE group moves into the situation to provide meals, to help with the details of the burial, and to stand beside the bereaved in comfort and concern. A telephone chain based upon the CARE groups is used to inform the congregation of special needs for prayer and ministry. More and more, the CARE group will be a small congregation where the individual has a consciousness of belonging, of being loved and encouraged in his growth in Christ.

The CARE groups are certainly not an answer to all the needs of the congregation. In fact, our hope is that the involvement there will simply be a catalyst to motivate people to even deeper involvement in personal discipleship and other small group involvements. Throughout our congregation there has been growing a commitment to be involved in the lives of other people. Some men meet for breakfast on the way to work. Ladies in the neighborhood come together for coffee and to pray and encourage one another. Some of these have become support groups where people with a particular kind of a burden or problem will meet together with others to find mutual encouragement. These kinds of relationships cannot be organized. They are the natural fruit of *koinonia.*

This small-group concept that is working effectively through our CARE groups has also become a model for our young adults and even our teenage youth groups. It has been our conviction that this kind of fellowship in which other people become comfortable verbalizing their life in Christ with each other tends to engender a growing witness in our community. When believers experience *koinonia,* and the love of Christ is shed abroad among them, an openness and witness is created in their larger community.

If we are serious about our call to witness in our culture then the church must equip the laity for witness. In evaluating the time investments and priorities of our leadership and staff, we began to see that we were giving little attention to this kind of equipping. This past year we added to our staff a pastor especially motivated and trained for evangelism.

The strategy decided upon was that of the Evangelism Explosion ministry developed by James Kennedy. In the spring of 1981 we formed three witness teams, each consisting of three individuals who committed themselves to seventeen weeks of intensive training which included visiting homes in our area to share the gospel of Jesus Christ in a clear and forthright way. This period of intensive training has produced a group of lay people enthused and motivated about their calling to be witnesses. In fall 1982 each of these is looking for two new disciples to be part of their team. We are hoping to have about nine teams this fall and, perhaps, over twenty by the first of the year. The vision is for this multiplying type of discipleship to permeate our congregation so that a large number of our people will be thoroughly trained to give a confident and clear answer for the reason of their hope in Christ.

This, however, is only one way that we are endeavoring to enable our people in their witness ministry. Evangelistic home Bible study has been another very fruitful avenue for our people to touch the lives of neighbors with an effective call to discipleship. Each summer, Long Hill sponsors what it calls a "Christian Workshop." Members of the congregation offer to teach classes in practical subjects. These include such things as arts and crafts, electronics, tennis, soccer, bicycle, and automobile repair. Each of these classes is presented along with a biblical lesson to demonstrate that every area of our life and giftedness is under the Lordship of Jesus Christ. The Workshop has been the means of building bridges of friendship all throughout our community through which our life in Jesus Christ can be shared in a very natural way.

No, we certainly have not arrived. No, every member is not an effective minister. However, the leadership of this congregation has adopted that ideal. We are seeking to bring all our priorities and time investments to work toward fulfillment of that goal.

BEING A SERVANT

I think that any pastor who has wrestled with the issue of being an enabler of the laity soon comes to the realization that the key to this ministry is being a certain kind of a person. Significant changes need to come about in the way that he sees himself and in his way of relating to other people.

Our traditional view of the clergy has been of a person somewhat aloof from the members of the congregation. One's authority and influence in the congregation was to be maintained by not letting anyone really see his personal weakness or inadequacy.

However, discipling people and giving one's ministry away involves a certain amount of vulnerability. One must be willing to be known as a man, as a sinner being saved by grace. If I want to say with the apostle Paul, "Follow me as I follow Christ," then I must let people see, in a rather intimate fashion, just how it is that I follow Christ. That is not always comfortable. Mark 3:14

says that Jesus chose twelve men to be with him. The pastor is God's spokesman. He has a divine calling to proclaim God's Word fearlessly and faithfully. He must not relinquish this stewardship. Yet, in the end, the growing of a church that becomes One People involves a pastor who is willing to be *with* his people.

Conclusion

It is very necessary for the health and vigor of the contemporary Church that it should recover the biblical emphasis which we have been exploring. The principles of it can no doubt be applied in a multitude of different ways. But the principles themselves are of permanent validity and cannot be changed. They are also closely related to each other and cannot be separated—at least not without resultant damage to the Church's life.

First, God's people are one holy people, owing their unity and holiness to the will and call of God himself. They are his *ecclesia,* called out to be his. As such, they are distinct from the world, but essentially undifferentiated from one another.

Next, in this one *ecclesia* God appoints different men and women to different ministries. Each has his particular *diakonia* to perform. And the principal service of the ordained ministry is to serve the rest of the Church, proclaiming Christ by word and sacrament, "warning every man and teaching every man in all wisdom, that we may present every man mature in Christ" (Colossians 1:28). So the clergy may say to the laity, *"Our* God-given *diakonia* in the Church is to help to equip you for *your* God-given *diakonia* in the world."

Further, although the *diakonia* of God's people (that is the laity) is varied, one of its highest forms is *marturia,* witness. Living and working in the midst of the secular world, the lay person is in the front line of the Church's testimony.

To this work of witness all God's people are summoned, and are regularly strengthened in the doing of it by their *koinonia,* their common share in Christian privilege and responsibility.

Select Bibliography

Some recent works, which relate to the theology of the laity and which are quoted in this book, are detailed below. They are listed in alphabetical order according to the authors' names. You are referred to this list also for works for which only brief details are given in the footnotes or the text.

Allan, Tom: *The Face Of My Parish* (SCM Press, 1954).

Bliss, Kathleen: *We The People, A Book About Laity* (SCM Press, 1963).

Chafin, Kenneth: *Help! I'm A Layman* (Word Books, 1966).

Garbett, Cyril: *The Claims Of The Church Of England* (Hodder and Stoughton, 1947).

Goyder, George: *The People's Church* (Hodder and Stoughton, 1966).

Green, Michael: *Called To Serve—Ministry and Ministers in the Church* (Hodder and Stoughton, 1964).

Grubb, Sir Kenneth: *A Layman Looks At the Church* (Hodder and Stoughton, 1964).

Kraemer, Hendrik: *A Theology Of The Laity* (Lutterworth, 1958).

Larson, Bruce: *Dare To Live Now!* (Michigan, Zondervan, 1965).

Miller, Keith: *The Taste Of New Wine* (Word Books, 1963).

Newbigin, Lesslie: *The Household Of God* (SCM Press, 1953).

Robinson, J. A. T. and others: *Layman's Church* (Lutterworth, 1963).

Robinson, J. A. T.: *The New Reformation?* (SCM Press, 1965).

Trueblood, Elton: *The Incendiary Fellowship* (Harper and Row, 1967).

Verney, Stephen: *Fire In Coventry* (Hodder and Stoughton, 1964).

Warren, M. A. C.: *Revival—An Enquiry* (SCM Press, 1954).

Reports (listed chronologically)

Towards the Conversion of England (Press and Publications Board of the Church Assembly, 1945).

The Evanston Report, the official report of the Second Assembly of the World Council of Churches (SCM Press, 1955).

The Lambeth Conference 1958 (SPCK, 1958).

Keele '67, the National Evangelical Anglican Congress Statement (Falcon, 1967).

The Documents of Vatican II, edited by Walter M. Abbott, S.J. (Geoffrey Chapman, 1967).

The Lambeth Conference 1968 (SPCK, 1968).

Notes

Introduction

1. Sir Kenneth Grubb, *A Layman Looks at the Church,* p. 161.
2. *The Lambeth Conference,* 1958, p. 1.26.
3. *Ibid.,* p. 2.99.
4. Tom Allan, *The Face of My Parish,* p. 54.
5. Hendrik Kraemer, *A Theology of the Laity,* pp. 34, 37.
6. Leslie Paul comments: "The revealing fact is that the laity have seldom been used in the past, and are seldom used by the Church today, in church affairs at the level of their ability in secular affairs" (*Layman's Church,* p. 43).
7. M.A.C. Warren, *Revival—An Enquiry,* p. 28.
8. Yves M.J. Congar, *Lay People in the Church* (English translation, 1957, p.13).

Chapter 1

1. For instance, Genesis 22:17, 18.
2. Genesis 50:26.
3. Hosea 11:1.
4. Exodus 19:4–6.
5. Jeremiah 16:14, 15.
6. 1 Corinthians 1:9; Romans 1:6.
7. 2 Timothy 1:9; 1 Thessalonians 4:7.
8. *See* 1 Peter 1:15, 16; Ephesians 4:1.
9. For instance, Romans 1:7; 1 Corinthians 1:2; *see also* Acts 15:14; Titus 2:14.
10. Lesslie Newbigin, *The Household of God,* pp. 31, 25—"eschatological," derived from *eschatos* ("last") or *eschaton* ("end"), refers to the end of time and the last things, the consummation which lies beyond history.
11. 1 Peter 2:9.
12. 1 Peter 2:20, 21; 5:10.
13. Ephesians 2:12.
14. Ephesians 2:13–16.
15. Galatians 3:28.
16. Romans 10:12, 13.
17. Colossians 3:11; Ephesians 2:19; 3:6.
18. No English translation can do justice to the striking Greek com-

pounds *sumpolitai,* fellow citizens; *sugkleronoma,* fellow heirs; *sussoma,* fellow members, and *summetocha,* fellow partakers.

19. For instance, Ezekiel 16; Jeremiah 2:2; 31:32; Isaiah 62:5.

20. For instance, Hosea 2.

21. Psalm 80:8–19; Isaiah 5.

22. Psalm 80:1; Isaiah 63:9; 40:11.

23. Mark 2:18–20.

24. *See* Ephesians 5:22–33.

25. Revelation 19:7; 21:2.

26. Mark 12.

27. John 15.

28. Luke 15:3–7; John 10.

29. Psalm 114:2.

30. Colossians 1:13.

31. Romans 14:17.

32. Hosea 11:1.

33. For instance, 1 John 2:29–3:3; 3:9, 10; Romans 8:14–17; Galatians 4:4–7.

34. Matthew 6:7–13, 25–34; 7:7–11.

35. 1 Corinthians 3:11, 16; Ephesians 2:20–22.

36. For instance, Ephesians 4:4, 15, 16; Colossians 2:19.

37. 1 Corinthians 12:14–26.

38. 2 Corinthians 11:2; John 3:29.

39. 1 Corinthians 3:5–15.

40. For instance, Acts 20:28; 1 Peter 5:1–4.

41. For instance, Acts 20:25; 1 Corinthians 4; 1 Thessalonians 2:7.

42. 1 Corinthians 12:21.

43. *See* 1 Peter 2:5, 9, 10.

Chapter 2

1. Leviticus 18:2–4.

2. Matthew 20:25, 26.

3. Ephesians 4:17.

4. "Ministry and laity are one. There may be a difference in function but there is no difference in essence" (Report of the Committee on "Progress in the Anglican Communion," *Lambeth Conference, 1958,* page 2.113).

5. Romans 12:4–6.

6. For instance, Acts 4:10—literally "all the people Israel."

7. For instance, Acts 15:14—"God ... visited the Gentiles, to take out of them a people for his name."

8. Luke 23:13; compare 20:19.

9. Acts 4:13.

10. Matthew 18:17.

11. 1 Corinthians 5:4, 5, 13.

12. Kraemer, *A Theology of the Laity*, p. 11.

13. Quoted in J. A. T. Robinson, *Layman's Church*, p. 10.

14. A quotation from the dustcover of Kenneth Chafin, *Help! I'm A Layman*.

15. Grubb, *A Layman Looks at the Church*, p. 26.

16. Article XXI, *Book of Common Prayer*, 1622.

17. Resolution 24 of the 1968 Lambeth Conference reads: "The Conference recommends that no major issue in the life of the Church should be decided without the full participation of the laity in discussion and in decision." For lack of this full participation of laity in their own conference the bishops admit that their report is not "the balanced document" they would have wished (p. 120).

18. Mark 10:42–44.

19. Kraemer, *A Theology of the Laity*, p. 146.

20. Philippians 2:7.

21. John 13:3–15.

22. Luke 22:24–27.

23. John 13:14, 15.

24. Michael Green: *Called to Serve—Ministry and Ministers in the Church*, p. 14.

25. 2 Corinthians 1:24; 1 Peter 5:3.

26. 1 Corinthians 3:5.

27. 1 Corinthians 4:1.

28. Acts 14:23.

29. Philippians 1:1.

30. Titus 1:5.

31. Ephesians 4:11.

32. 1 Thessalonians 5:12, 13.

33. 1 Timothy 3:5, 12.

34. The verb is *kopiao* in both verses, meaning "to toil."

35. This is the plural participle *hoi hegoumenoi humon* in Hebrews

13:7, 17, 24; compare Acts 15:22 where the expression is used of Judas Barsabbas and Silas.

36. Acts 7:10.

37. Matthew 2:6.

38. Luke 22:26—*"ho hegoumenos hos ho diakonon."*

39. Hebrews 13:17; 1 Corinthians 16:16.

40. Hebrews 13:7.

41. Acts 20:28; 1 Peter 5:2.

42. 3 John 9.

43. *The Documents of Vatican II*, p. 486.

44. *Vatican II*, p. 58.

45. *Vatican II*, p. 64.

46. *Vatican II*, p. 40.

47. *Vatican II*, p. 56.

48. *Vatican II*, p. 57.

49. *Vatican II*, p. 96.

50. Kathleen Bliss, *We The People, A Book About Laity*, p. 87.

51. W. Robinson, *Completing The Reformation, The Doctrine of The Priesthood Of All Believers* (Lexington, Kentucky: College of the Bible, 1955).

52. Hebrews 10:21.

53. Revelation 1:6, 5:10; 20:6.

54. 1 Peter 2:5.

55. Kraemer, *A Theology of the Laity*, p. 34.

56. For Anglican teaching on laymen as ministers of Word and Sacrament from the Reformation to 1662, see R. T. Beckwith, *Priesthood and Sacraments* (Marcham, 1964), pp. 42–46; for Bishop J. A. T. Robinson's outspoken criticism of what he calls "the clergy line" and the false "mystique" or "semi-magical status" often attributed to clergy, *see The New Reformation?*, pp. 56, 57.

57. *Book of Common Prayer*, 1662.

58. "Errand-boys" is a popular version of *diakonoi* which I once heard used by Canon Leon Morris, Principal of Ridley College, Melbourne.

59. 2 Corinthians 4:5.

60. Luke 22:26.

61. Titus 2:14; compare 1 Peter 2:9—*laos periousios.*

62. Acts 15:14.

63. 1 Peter 2:9.

64. 1 Corinthians 12:5.

65. Chafin, *Help! I'm A Layman*, p. 25.

66. Kraemer, *A Theology of the Laity*, p. 181.

67. Robinson, *Layman's Church*, p. 18; in *The New Reformation?* he writes of "almost total immersion" in the world, p. 69.

68. Kraemer, *A Theology of the Laity*, p. 174.

69. Grubb, *A Layman Looks at the Church*, pp. 30, 31, 34.

70. 1 Timothy 3:2; compare 2 Timothy 2:24.

71. Titus 1:9.

72. As the Swiss ecumenical leader Hans-Ruedi Weber has expressed it: "The laity are not helpers of the clergy so that the clergy can do their job, but the clergy are helpers of the whole people of God, so that the laity can be the Church." This is quoted by Robinson both in *Layman's Church* (p. 17) and in *The New Reformation?* (p. 55). He also quotes from Gibson Winter, *The New Creation as Metropolis:* "The ministry is usually conceived today as the work of clergymen with auxiliary aids among the laity; ministry in the servant Church is the work of laity in the world with auxiliary help from theological specialists" (*The New Reformation?*, p. 65).

73. Bliss, *We The People*, p. 69.

74. 1 Corinthians 3:21, 22.

Chapter 3

1. Luke 22:27.

2. John 13:14–16.

3. Gustaf Wingren, *The Living Word* (Sweden, 1949; English edition, SCM Press, 1960), p. 104.

4. Ephesians 6:4.

5. Acts 1:8.

6. John 15:26, 27.

7. Elton Trueblood, *The Incendiary Fellowship*, p. 36.

8. Especially Robert Raines, *New Life in the Church* (Harper and Row, 1963) and Thomas Mullen, *The Renewal of the Ministry* (Abingdon, 1963).

9. Trueblood, *The Incendiary Fellowship*, p. 41.

10. *Ibid.*, p. 42.

11. *Ibid.*, p. 143.

12. Keith Miller, *The Taste of New Wine*, pp. 111–113.

13. *Towards the Conversion of England*, p. 36.

14. Cyril Garbett, *The Claims of the Church of England*, p. 177.

15. *The Evanston Report*, p. 103.

16. Colossians 1:28.

17. *Keele '67*, p. 23, para. 20.

18. Galatians 5:13.

19. For instance, Romans 12:13.

Chapter 4

1. See Genesis 2:18.

2. M. E. Macdonald, *The Need to Believe* (Fontana, 1959), p. 82.

3. Bruce Larson, *Dare To Live Now!*, p. 110.

4. For instance, Romans 16:3–5; Philemon 1, 2.

5. Quoted in Leslie F. Church, *The Early Methodist People* (Epworth, 1948), p. 155.

6. Quoted by Church, *Ibid.*, p. 153.

7. C. H. Dodd, *Moffatt Commentary on the Johannine Epistles* (Hodder and Stoughton, 1946), p. 6.

8. Titus 1:4; Jude 3; Philippians 1:7.

9. Ephesians 2:8, 9.

10. 1 John 1:1–4; compare Acts 2:42.

11. 1 John 1:6, 7.

12. 1 Corinthians 1:9; 10:16; compare 10:20.

13. 2 Corinthians 13:14; Philippians 2:1; 2 Peter 1:4.

14. Ephesians 5:11; compare 2 Corinthians 6:14; Matthew 23:30; 1 Timothy 5:22; 2 John 11; Revelation 18:4.

15. Philippians 3:10 (KJV); 1 Peter 4:13; 5:1; Revelation 1:9; compare 2 Corinthians 1:7; Hebrews 10:33.

16. Hebrews 2:3.

17. Luke 5:10.

18. 2 Corinthians 8:23; Philemon 6, 17.

19. Philippians 1:5; compare 1 Corinthians 9:23.

20. 1 Timothy 6:18.

21. Hebrews 13:16, "Do not neglect ... to share what you have" (RSV).

22. Romans 12:13.

23. Romans 15:26; 2 Corinthians 8:4, 9:13.

24. Quoted in Church, *The Early Methodist People,* p. 149.

25. Philippians 4:15.

26. Mutual Responsibility and Interdependence, a cumbrous expression for the reciprocal aid recommended to the churches by the Anglican Congress at Toronto in 1963.

27. Acts 2:44 (*hapanta koina*); compare Acts 4:32.

28. Compare Galatians 6:6; 1 Corinthians 9:11.

29. Romans 15:26, 27; compare Romans 11:7.

30. For instance, 2 Corinthians 7:6; 2 Timothy 4:9, 11, 21.

31. Romans 1:11, 12.

32. John 13:34, 35; 15:12, 17.

33. Romans 12:10; 13:8; 1 Thessalonians 3:12; 4:9; 1 Peter 1:22; 1 John 3:11, 23; 4:7, 11, 12; 2 John 5.

34. Romans 14:13; Galatians 5:15, 26; Colossians 3:9; James 4:11; 5:9.

35. Romans 14:19; 15:7; Ephesians 4:2, 32; Colossians 3:13; Galatians 5:13 (compare John 13:14); 1 Peter 4:9; Romans 15:14; Ephesians 5:21; 1 Peter 5:5; 1 Thessalonians 4:18.

36. Romans 12:5; compare Ephesians 4:25.

37. 1 Corinthians 12:25, 26.

38. Romans 16:16; 1 Corinthians 16:20; 2 Corinthians 13:12; 1 Peter 5:14.

39. Hebrews 10:24, 25.

40. James 5:16.

41. Galatians 6:2; Romans 12:15.

42. Trueblood, *The Incendiary Fellowship,* p. 31.

43. *Ibid.,* p. 83.

44. Larson, *Dare to Live Now!,* p. 122.

45. Quoted in J. S. Simon, *John Wesley and the Methodist Societies* (1923).